T0243781

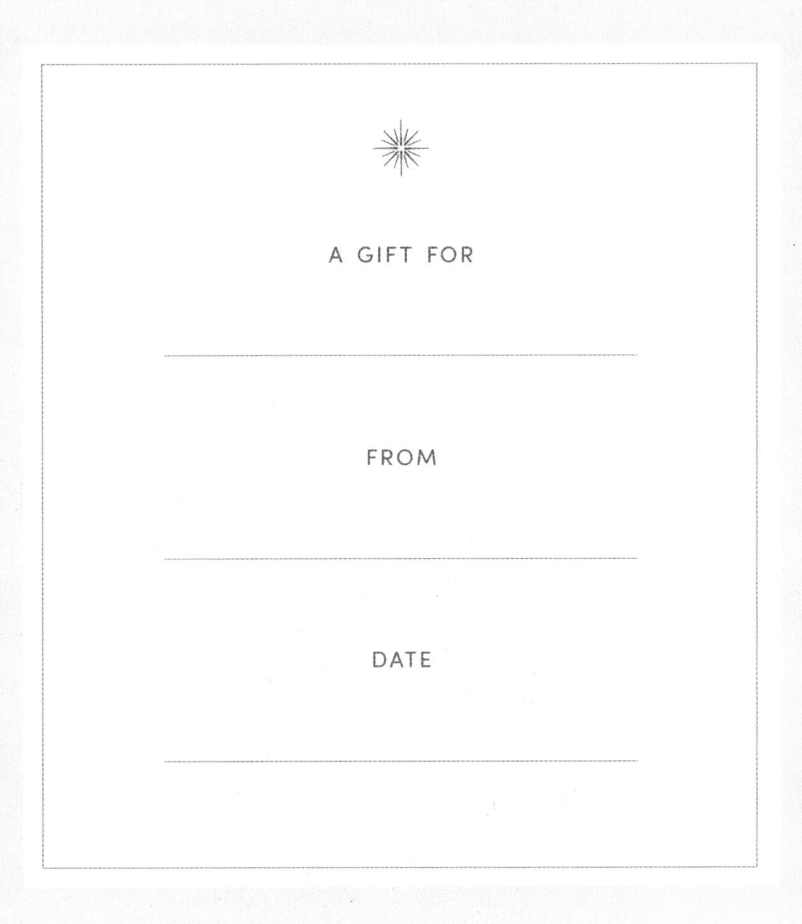
A GIFT FOR
FROM
DATE

Gifts & Gratitudes

A YEAR OF
ONE THOUSAND GIFTS

A JOURNAL

ANN VOSKAMP

THOMAS NELSON
Since 1798

Gifts & Gratitudes

Text in this book has been excerpted from *One Thousand Gifts* (Thomas Nelson 2011)

Published in Nashville, Tennessee, by Thomas Nelson. Thomas Nelson is a registered trademark of HarperCollins Christian Publishing, Inc.

Published in association with William K. Jensen Literary Agency, 119 Bampton Court, Eugene, Oregon 97404.

Cover Design: Michelle Lenger

Interior Design: Kristen Sasamoto

Photos: Ann Voskamp, from her own counting of gifts

Thomas Nelson titles may be purchased in bulk for educational, business, fund-raising, or sales promotional use. For information, please email SpecialMarkets@ThomasNelson.com.

ISBN 978-1-4002-4995-4 (HC)

Printed in Malaysia

24 25 26 27 28 COS 10 9 8 7 6 5 4 3 2 1

To my grandchildren. Each of your parents have been the most astonishing, flattening grace—and each of you are simply, delightfully, grace upon grace.

Amma is smitten with the gift of each of you.

Introduction

It all began quite spontaneously, unintentionally—one of those things God grows up in the most unexpected places.

A friend dared me to start counting one thousand things I loved. I took the dare, accepted the challenge, kept track of one thousand things, one thousand gifts—a thousand *graces*—on a quiet, unassuming blog. Before I knew it, thankfulness to God began to fully change me.

I found more daily wonder and surprising beauty than I ever expected. And in a few short years, this daily hunt for God's grace ushered me into a fuller life. A life of joy! Over the past several years, I've listed thousands of gifts, and I continue and won't ever stop because the gifts never end. Hundreds of thousands more have begun their own lists—in jail cells and by deathbeds, in third-world slums and by faith alone—and it's not an overstatement to say that giving Him thanks has made me and innumerable others *overcomers*.

Through this intentional, daily practice of giving thanks, I found myself on a transformative journey that affected every aspect of my life, including all the broken places. God began to show me the graces, the love gifts, that were right before me, waiting to be noticed, waiting to be received. This easily overlooked stuff, the small—and especially the hard—became for me a life-giving stream of *joy in Him.*

Even when impatient or unwilling, when facing conflict or deepest heartache, I've begun to accept that even in the impossible, there still is an opportunity to experience the goodness and gifts and grace of the Giver of all.

There is always only more grace.

And it's always more than you might expect.

In the midst of the mire, perhaps there is a way to think about counting one thousand gifts, about making your life, even now, especially now, still about joy in Christ, about loving God and enjoying Him forever. There is so much joy in seeing how He uses our simple act of *noticing* the blessings He bestows all around us to transform our lives and the lives of those we touch.

Maybe the way through, maybe the way to begin this journey by grace, of beginning your own gift list and counting all the ways He loves you, starts here:

Pray. Start with an honest request, making it the refrain of your tender days: "God, open the eyes of my heart." This journey is always Spirit-led, every day.

Receive. Open your hands to receive the unexpected, simple, daily gifts, writing down all the unique and ordinary things you notice, from the grand and obvious to the humble and hidden. God holds space for our heartache—and we get to hold space for His graces in the midst of our heartaches.

Praise. Praise Him for the unlikely, for the daily and the difficult, all the graces in disguise. The more you count, the more gifts you see. And honestly, do not disdain the small, because all the moments add up, and it's possible to believe it in a broken world—*the whole earth is full of His glory!*

I found that setting this goal of looking for one thousand gifts kept me attending to all the ways He kept whispering, "I love you." The practice of counting gifts is intended to be a way of cultivating a habit, of learning to live a life of authentic worship, of making gratitude and joy the soul's default, of moving thanksgiving away from a holiday to a *lifestyle*—such that all the days might be holy and set apart for living in the real presence of God.

But then, after more than a decade of counting gifts, when I discovered a new, fresh way of practicing this, I was, frankly, beyond ecstatic—it turned out to be absolutely life-changing!

Reimagining a gratitude journal, with a page for each day of the month, and then creating space on each day of the month's page for each month of the year, has yielded a miraculous gift. You get the opportunity to reflect on all the gifts you've recorded on this day in previous months!

Just every day, record a few gifts on that date of the month, and then the next day, turn the page and write down a few more gifts for that day.

Keep counting gifts every day of the month, and every day you get the gift of seeing all the ways God's gifted you grace upon grace, every day, over the course of the year!

What I've discovered in doing this has changed my life: The more opportunities you have to remember the goodness and graces of God, the more the broken places in your heart and story are literally re-membered. Remember more of God's goodness, and more of your brokenness is re-membered.

I discovered that this fresh new way of counting gifts and gratitudes builds in a daily way to remember how God's provided on this day in past months—which grows your trust in God to provide yet again for today and all the days to come!

Each day of the month includes short reflections on living an authentic practice of gratitude, which you can read if you have time that day, or if you're running short on time, you can rest easy, as you have twelve opportunities across the course of the year to read that day of the month's gratitude reflection. My sincere prayer is that these glimpses will gently accompany you in your own prayerful, honest discovery of a lifestyle of genuine thankfulness that is the door into the fullest life.

It's an invitation: when there's a daily, brave scavenger hunt for gifts, a bit of every complicated day finds itself salvaged.

It's life-changing: count the gifts and grace of God, and you discover you can count on God.

It's possible: God never stops catching every one of our tender tears in a bottle. What if we never stopped counting every one of His graces in a book of our own?

This is your own book of gifts and gratitudes—a record of your amazing life and His amazing grace.

ALL IS GRACE.

Ann

But who am I, and who are my people? . . . Everything comes from you, and we have given you only what comes from your hand.

1 CHRONICLES 29:14

1

grace glimpse

Surprising Grace

And this is the law of the sacrifice of peace offerings that one may offer to the LORD. If he offers it for a thanksgiving, then he shall offer with the thanksgiving sacrifice unleavened loaves mixed with oil, unleavened wafers smeared with oil, and loaves of fine flour well mixed with oil. With the sacrifice of his peace offerings for thanksgiving he shall bring his offering with loaves of leavened bread.

LEVITICUS 7:11–13 ESV

Surprisingly, the first time thanksgiving is ever mentioned in Scripture, it's to note that the thanksgiving offering is part of the peace offering.

Could it be thatno one receives the peace of God without giving thanks to God? Is thankfulness really but the deep, contented breath of peacefulness? Is this why God asks us to look for glimpses of grace to give thanks for even when things look dark? When there doesn't seem to be much to give thanks for?

There were to be ten offerings of bread in every thank offering of the Israelites. The first were like crackers. The second like wafers. These were known for their thinness. This was the order of thanks. The thanks began for the thin things, the wafer things that almost weren't, and the way the people of God gave thanks was first to give thanks for even the meager and unlikely.

Then it came, thanks for the leavened bread. Why would leaven, yeast—that which is seen in Scripture as impure, unwanted—be included as part of the thank offering?

God always holds space for all our authentic lament. He then invites us to make space for authentic thanks through all things, because our God is a God kneading *all* things into a bread that sustains. To bring the sacrifice of thanksgiving means thanking God for everything because He is benevolent. A sacrifice of thanks lays down our perspective and raises hands both in honest lament and heartfelt praise—*always*. A sacrifice is, by definition, not an easy thing—but it is a sacred thing.

There is this: We give thanks to God not because of how we feel but because of who He is. It's counting the ways He still loves. *This* is what keeps multiplying joy.

The life that keeps counting blessings discovers it's yielding more beauty than it seems.

God, move me to know it afresh today: the life that counts blessings discovers it's yielding much more beauty than it seems. And my life yields most when I yield most to You.

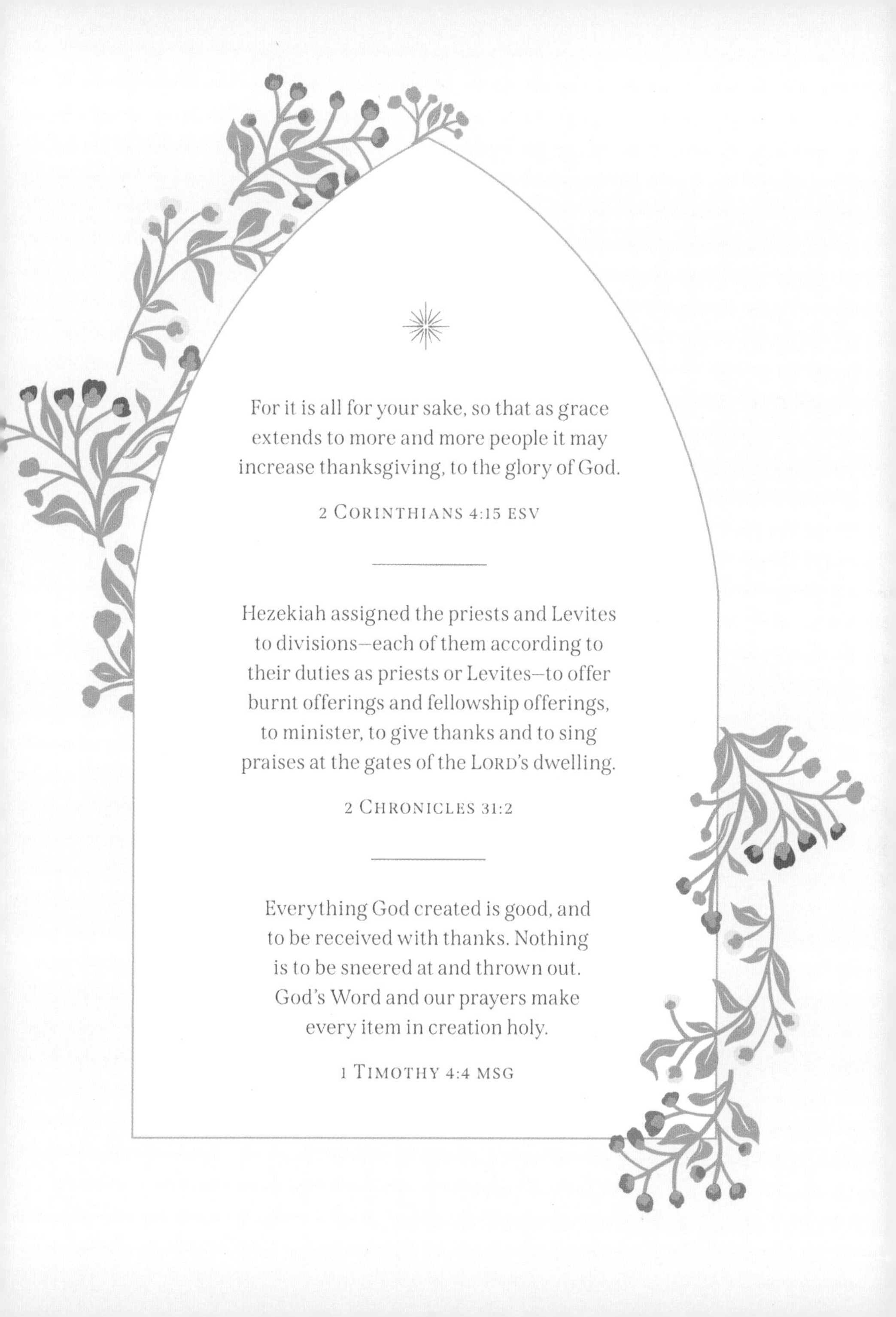

For it is all for your sake, so that as grace extends to more and more people it may increase thanksgiving, to the glory of God.

2 CORINTHIANS 4:15 ESV

Hezekiah assigned the priests and Levites to divisions—each of them according to their duties as priests or Levites—to offer burnt offerings and fellowship offerings, to minister, to give thanks and to sing praises at the gates of the LORD's dwelling.

2 CHRONICLES 31:2

Everything God created is good, and to be received with thanks. Nothing is to be sneered at and thrown out. God's Word and our prayers make every item in creation holy.

1 TIMOTHY 4:4 MSG

Gifts & Gratitudes

JANUARY

#

#

#

FEBRUARY

#

#

#

MARCH

#

#

#

APRIL

#

#

#

MAY

#

#

#

JUNE

#

#

#

1ST

JULY

#

#

#

AUGUST

#

#

#

SEPTEMBER

#

#

#

OCTOBER

#

#

#

NOVEMBER

#

#

#

DECEMBER

#

#

#

Then the people rejoiced because they had given willingly,
for with a whole heart they had offered freely to the LORD.

1 CHRONICLES 29:9 ESV

2

grace glimpse

Choosing Grace

His secret purpose framed from the very beginning [is] to bring us to our full glory.

1 CORINTHIANS 2:7 NEB

Everywhere you look, it's so easy to see a world pocked with scarcity. And you hunger for soul-filling in a world that is starved.

But from that garden beginning, God has had a different purpose for you. Open the Bible and there are His plans, and His love letter to us forever silences any doubts: He means to rename us—to return us to our true names, our truest selves. "God's wisdom is something mysterious that goes deep into the interior of his purposes. You don't find it lying around on the surface. It's not the latest message, but more like the oldest—what God determined as the way to bring out his best in us" (1 Corinthians 2:7 MSG).

From the very beginning, that Eden beginning, this has always been and continues to be His secret purpose: our return to *our full glory,* to bring out His best in us. Us! And yet since we took a bite out of the fruit and tore into our own souls, God's had this wild secretive plan. In the midst of everything: *He means to fill us with glory again*. With glory and grace.

Grace means "favor," from the Latin *gratia*. It connotes a free readiness. That's grace: a free and ready *favor.*

It is one thing to choose to take the grace offered at the cross. But to choose to live as one daily *filling* with His grace? Choosing to daily *fill* with *all* that He freely gives, and to fully live—with glory and grace and God? God's grace upon grace, God's favor upon free and ready favor.

Much of life comes like a river: it can't be controlled or tamed. And, too, much of life is about choosing to resist—or choosing to receive.

While living through losses, there is still a tender choice to say yes to receiving what He gives and trusting there are gifts and grace even here.

God of all gifts, thank You. Thank You! For the grace to choose to see. I choose to say yes today to all You give. Do the work in me—I want to more fully live.

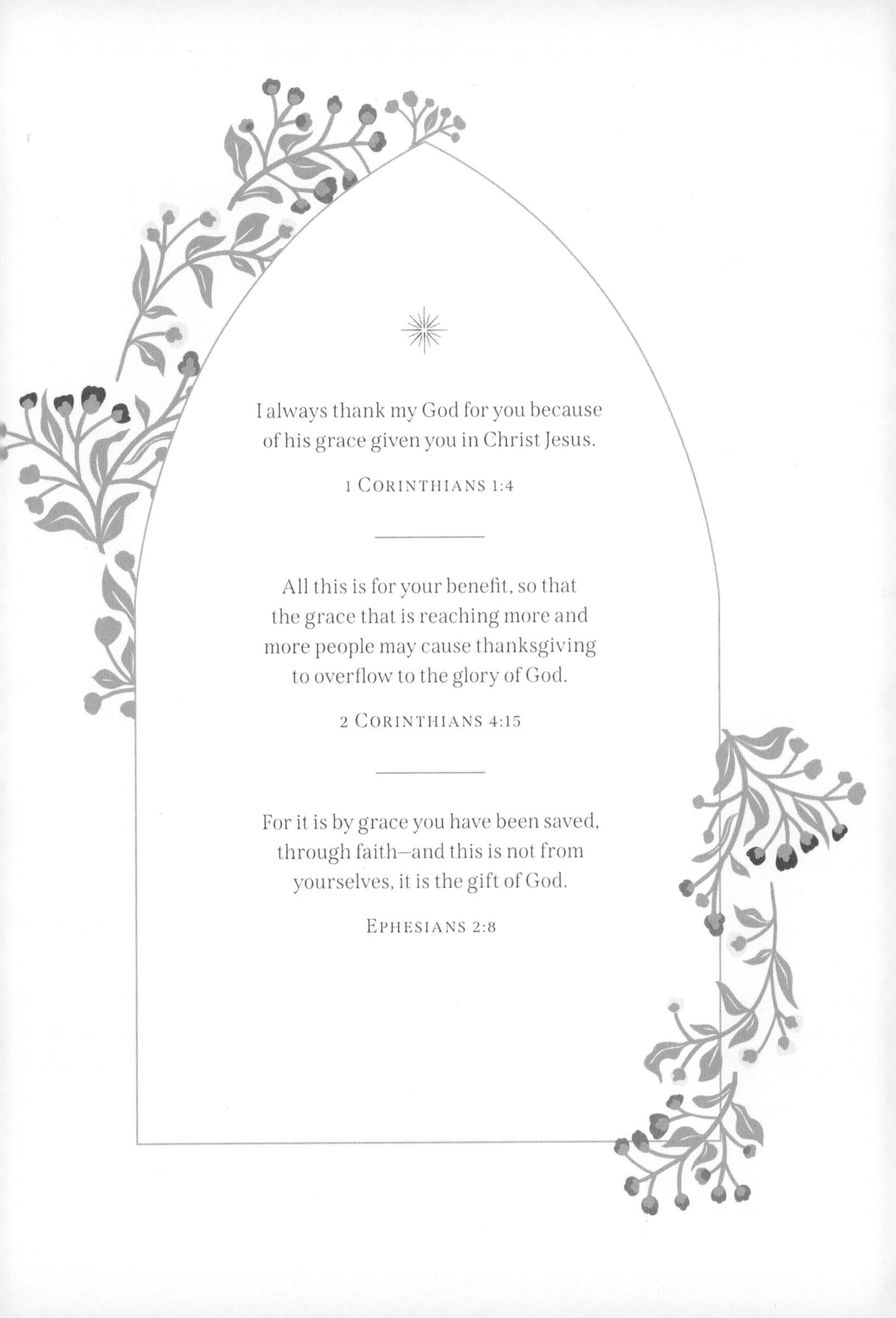

I always thank my God for you because of his grace given you in Christ Jesus.

1 CORINTHIANS 1:4

All this is for your benefit, so that the grace that is reaching more and more people may cause thanksgiving to overflow to the glory of God.

2 CORINTHIANS 4:15

For it is by grace you have been saved, through faith—and this is not from yourselves, it is the gift of God.

EPHESIANS 2:8

Gifts & Gratitudes

JANUARY

#
#
#

FEBRUARY

#
#
#

MARCH

#
#
#

APRIL

#
#
#

MAY

#
#
#

JUNE

#
#
#

2ND

JULY

#

#

#

AUGUST

#

#

#

SEPTEMBER

#

#

#

OCTOBER

#

#

#

NOVEMBER

#

#

#

DECEMBER

#

#

#

Give thanks in all circumstances; for this is God's will for you in Christ Jesus.

1 THESSALONIANS 5:18

3

grace glimpse

First Grace

But the basic reality of God is plain enough. Open your eyes and there it is! By taking a long and thoughtful look at what God has created, people have always been able to see what their eyes as such can't see: . . . the mystery of his divine being.

ROMANS 1:19–20 MSG

"First, I thank my God." That's what it reads, right there in Romans 1, the Farmer reading the words slowly aloud after dinner one evening, and it strikes me. Is that what that means? Thanksgiving, for at least something, anything, should always come first before everything else. Paul went on to write holy words that move me in convicting ways:

> The wrath of God is being revealed from heaven against all the godlessness. . . . For since the creation of the world God's invisible qualities—his eternal power and divine nature—have been clearly

seen, being understood from what has been made, so that people are without excuse.

For although they knew God, they neither glorified him as God nor gave thanks to him. . . . as they did not think it worthwhile to retain the knowledge of God, so God gave them over. (Romans 1:18, 20–21, 28)

One of the kindest friends and finest writers I know, Mark Buchanan, asked critical questions: "What initially sparks God's anger? What is the root sin . . . ?"[1] What cracks the heart of God, who is Love Himself?

It's right there in Romans 1. It's not sinfulness but our thanklessness that first breaks the very heart of God.

That reframes what it means to fall and fail throughout the day: our fall is always first a failure to give thanks.

I linger long here, moved and convicted in humbling, tender ways that are part of healing.

Because the reality of this world is this: if all the brokenness in the world begins with an act of forgettingto give thanks—then the act of remembering to give thanks to God begins to literally re-member us and all our broken places.

Remembering to give thanks re-members us from brokenness toward wholeness.

Father God, You are the Begetter of grace. Forgive me for being a forgetter of thanks. Hear the cry of my heart: Forgive me for not giving You thanks. If thanks is the highest form of thought—make it my first thought. Turn me toward You first—always.

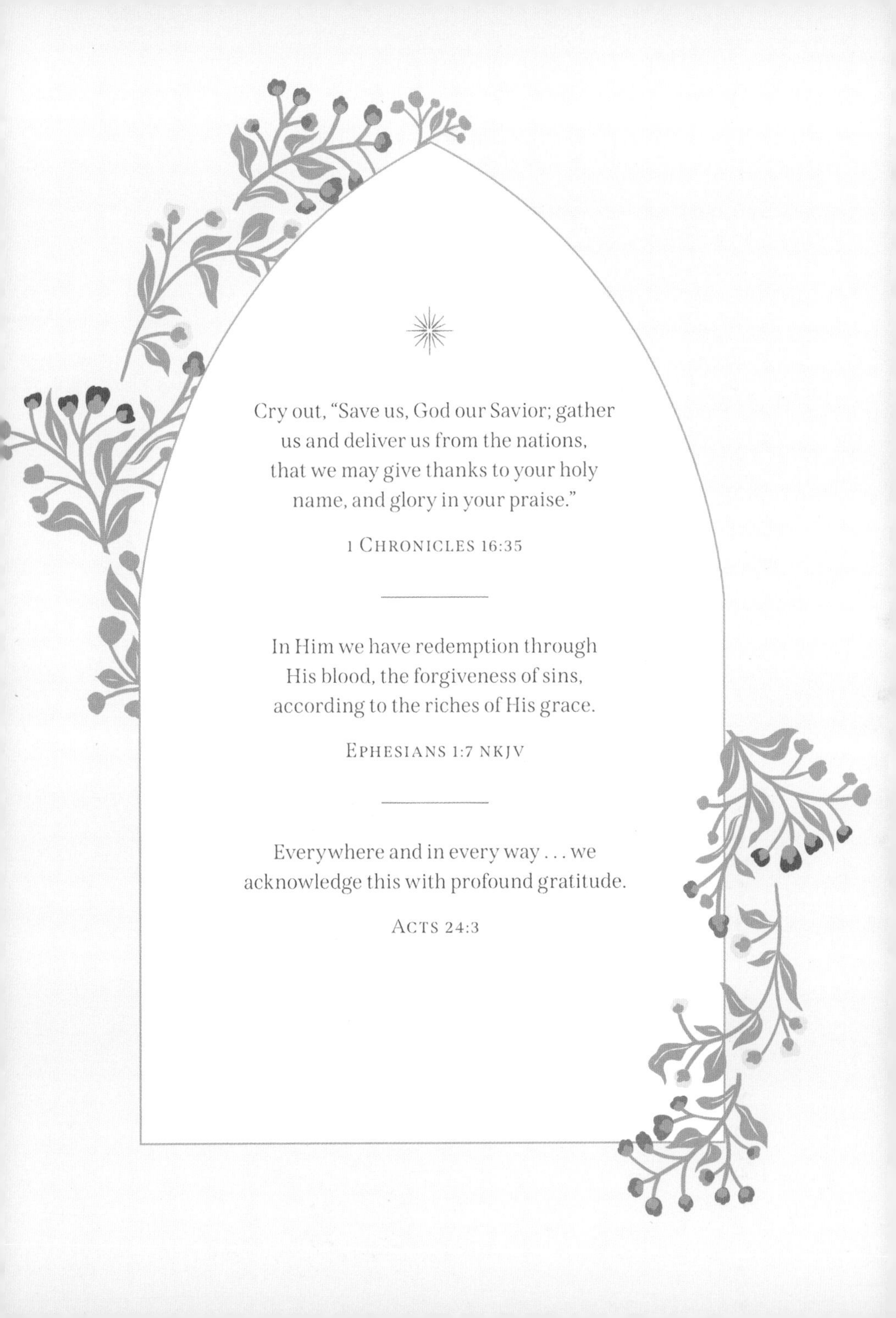

Cry out, “Save us, God our Savior; gather
us and deliver us from the nations,
that we may give thanks to your holy
name, and glory in your praise.”

1 CHRONICLES 16:35

In Him we have redemption through
His blood, the forgiveness of sins,
according to the riches of His grace.

EPHESIANS 1:7 NKJV

Everywhere and in every way . . . we
acknowledge this with profound gratitude.

ACTS 24:3

Gifts & Gratitudes

JANUARY

#

#

#

FEBRUARY

#

#

#

MARCH

#

#

#

APRIL

#

#

#

MAY

#

#

#

JUNE

#

#

#

3RD

JULY

#

#

#

AUGUST

#

#

#

SEPTEMBER

#

#

#

OCTOBER

#

#

#

NOVEMBER

#

#

#

DECEMBER

#

#

#

We will not hide them from their descendants; we will tell the next generation the praiseworthy deeds of the LORD, his power, and the wonders he has done.

PSALM 78:4

4

grace glimpse

Thinking Grace

Through Jesus, therefore, let us continually offer to God a sacrifice of praise—the fruit of lips that openly profess his name.

HEBREWS 13:15

I still think about it, how I can still see my son Levi in my mind's eye. He's all snow-caked from playing out in the drifts and I can hear his laughter falling like snow, his cheeks winter red, and his father winks at me as I fall back to lie on the snow, the moment warming me right through.

And I had tried to memorize all the wonderful—the faith and the falls and the fully living.

It's not trite, this waking to wonder, this giving thanks for all the beauty of living, even in the midst of all that's brutal.

Thanks isn't shallow Pollyannaism. Isn't that what Chesterton was suggesting?

"I would maintain that thanks are the highest form of thought, and that gratitude is happiness doubled by wonder."[1]

Thanks is the highest form of thought because to give thanks you must look up, through everything, to still see the love of the Giver on High. This takes moving higher up and deeper into the heart of God.

Those engaged in the highest thoughts are those who keep it at the forefront of their minds: how could I give thanks to God on High, even now?

This is what the great thinkers do—they stay awake to the wonder of God's world, the miracles in this moment, the glimpses of light prying through the dark.

This is a wounded world and there are valleys of ache at every turn, but all of life turns on the turn, and the art of really living is to keep turning in ways that keep you awake to the wonders in His Word, and to all the unexpected places in this tender world.

There is a way to practice smiling thanks for the wonder of here, to be in awed, childlike wonder for the most minute of moments, the kingdom of heaven belonging to those who are like the wide-eyed, delighted children.

If it's true, as writers and philosophers claim, that to think is to thank, then you know you're truly thinking deeply when you're truly thanking deeply.

Father God, make me never tire of the highest form of thinking—thanking. Make today great—by causing me to think gratefully. Engage me in the highest thoughts—gratefully laid low before You.

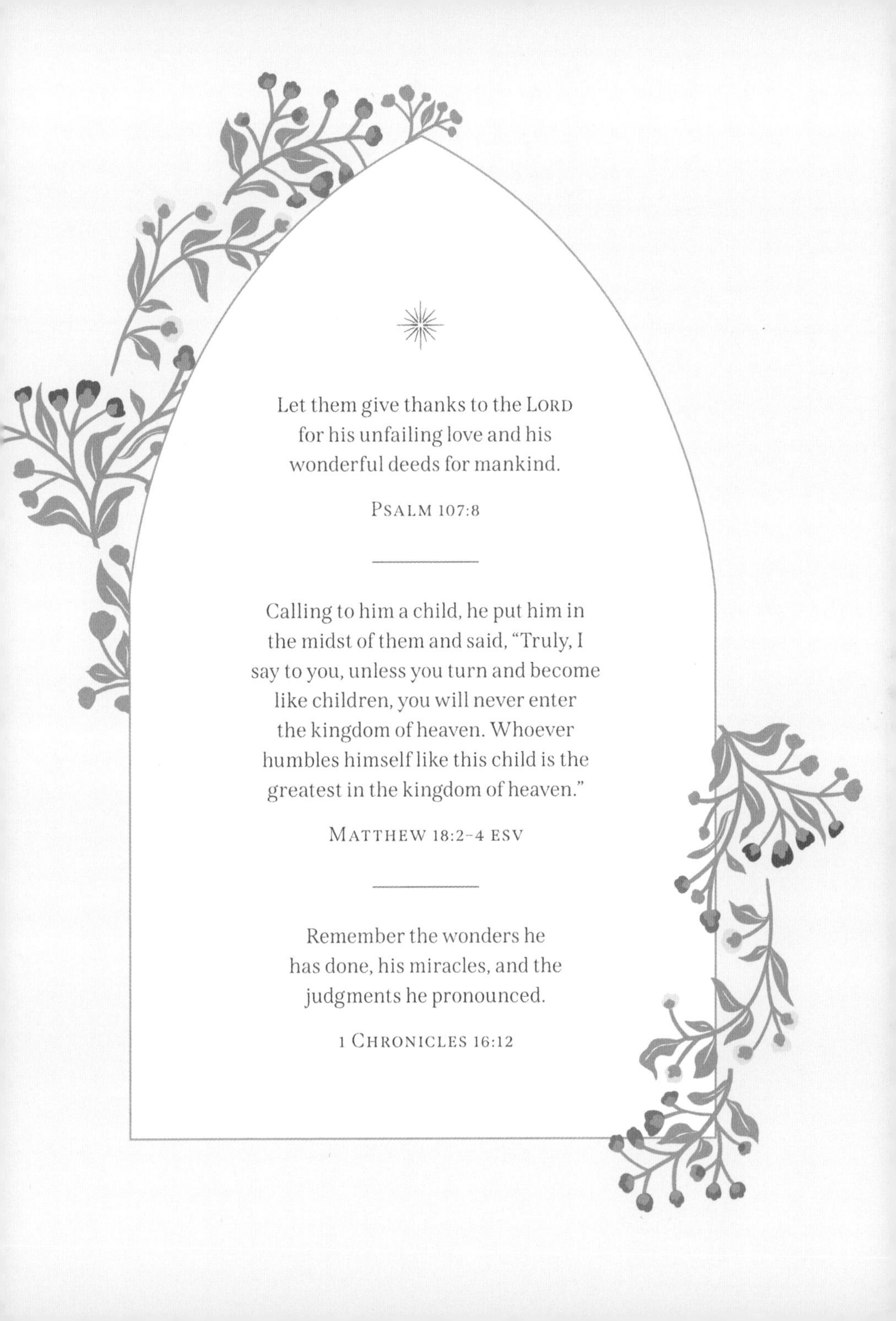

Let them give thanks to the LORD
for his unfailing love and his
wonderful deeds for mankind.

PSALM 107:8

Calling to him a child, he put him in
the midst of them and said, "Truly, I
say to you, unless you turn and become
like children, you will never enter
the kingdom of heaven. Whoever
humbles himself like this child is the
greatest in the kingdom of heaven."

MATTHEW 18:2–4 ESV

Remember the wonders he
has done, his miracles, and the
judgments he pronounced.

1 CHRONICLES 16:12

Gifts & Gratitudes

JANUARY

#

#

#

FEBRUARY

#

#

#

MARCH

#

#

#

APRIL

#

#

#

MAY

#

#

#

JUNE

#

#

#

4TH

JULY

#

#

#

AUGUST

#

#

#

SEPTEMBER

#

#

#

OCTOBER

#

#

#

NOVEMBER

#

#

#

DECEMBER

#

#

#

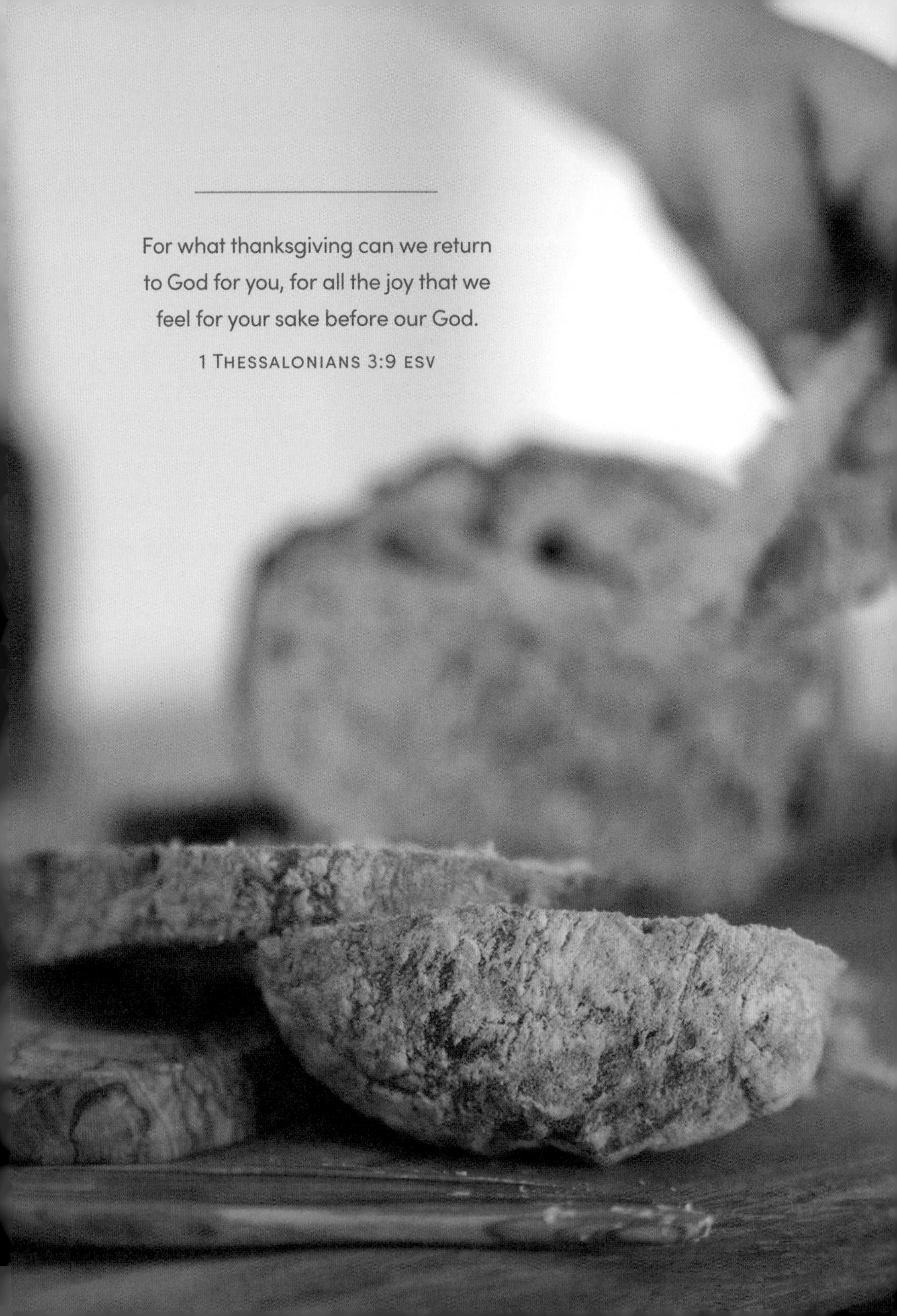

For what thanksgiving can we return to God for you, for all the joy that we feel for your sake before our God.

1 Thessalonians 3:9 ESV

5

grace glimpse

Here-Now Grace

And he took bread, gave thanks and broke it, and gave it to them.

LUKE 22:19

On the night He was betrayed, with an expiration of less than twelve hours, what did Jesus count as paramount?

"And he took bread, *gave thanks* and broke it, and gave it to them" (Luke 22:19, emphasis added).

I read it slowly, again and again. In the original language, "he gave thanks" reads "*eucharisteo*." I underline it on the page.

The root word of *eucharisteo* is *charis*, meaning "grace." Jesus took the bread and saw it as grace and gave thanks.

But there is more. *Eucharisteo*, thanksgiving, envelops the Greek word for grace, *charis*. But it also holds its derivative, the Greek word *chara*, meaning "joy." *Joy*. Ah . . . yes.

I breathe deep, like a sojourner finally coming home. This has always been the goal of the fullest life—*joy.* Who doesn't long for more *holy joy*?

But where can you seize this holy grail of joy?

That's what it says right there on the holy page: deep *chara* joy is found only at the table of the *euCHARisteo*—the table of thanksgiving.

There it is: the height of your *chara* joy is dependent on the depths of your *eucharisteo* thanks.

Which is to say: As long as thanks is possible—then joy is always possible. Joy is always possible.

I whisper it out loud.

Charis. Grace.

Eucharisteo. Thanksgiving.

Chara. Joy.

This is a threefold cord that is a lifeline, tethered to the heart of God.

God, thank You for showing me the beauty in all these here-now wonders You've placed before me—to do good and right work in me. Cause me to see all that encircles me today with new eyes of thankfulness.

And he took bread, gave thanks and broke it, and gave it to them, saying, "This is my body given for you; do this in remembrance of me."

LUKE 22:19

Now, our God, we give you thanks, and praise your glorious name.

1 CHRONICLES 29:13

I will sing for joy in GOD, explode in praise from deep in my soul!

ISAIAH 61:10 MSG

Gifts & Gratitudes

JANUARY

#

#

#

FEBRUARY

#

#

#

MARCH

#

#

#

APRIL

#

#

#

MAY

#

#

#

JUNE

#

#

#

5TH

JULY

#

#

#

AUGUST

#

#

#

SEPTEMBER

#

#

#

OCTOBER

#

#

#

NOVEMBER

#

#

#

DECEMBER

#

#

#

And rejoice! Celebrate all the good things that GOD, your God, has given you and your family.

DEUTERONOMY 26:11 MSG

6

grace glimpse

Anti-Anxiety Grace

I have certainly soothed and quieted my soul; like a weaned child resting against his mother, my soul within me is like a weaned child.

PSALM 131:2 NASB

John Calvin and I, we both remember the year we were four.

The year I was four, my sister Aimee was killed by a truck in our driveway. That is my first memory.

Fears have formed me.

John Calvin's mother died the year he was four. Calvin buried all three babies born to him and his wife. Scholar and historian William Bouwsma described Calvin as "a singularly anxious man."[1]

What might somewhat alleviate some complicated anxiousness in a complicated world of unknowns? Calvin wrote, "The stability of the world depends on this rejoicing of God in His works. . . . If on earth, such praise of God does not come to pass, . . . then the whole order of nature will be thrown into confusion."[2]

In a confusing world, our interior world can reel unless we rejoice, and a song of thanks can steady much more than you imagine. In the midst of many needful and thoughtful approaches to anxiousness, this is one possibility: deep anxiousness may find deep comfort in deep adoration of Christ.

"We are cold when it comes to rejoicing in God!" wrote Calvin. "Hence, we need to exercise ourselves in it and employ all our senses in it—our feet, our hands, our arms and all the rest—that they all might serve in the worship of God and so magnify Him."[3]

There's always this invitation to exercise: to pick up a pen, write down a few more gifts—*employ* the senses to see and hear and inhale and taste the grace and gifts and goodness of God.

Your sense of joy can grow stronger when you exercise your senses to taste and see unexpected ways to keep exercising your gratitude muscle.

Much exaltation of Christ can bring much comfort to much anxiousness.

Holy Father, John Calvin said the stability of the world depends on the rejoicing in Your works. Doesn't my world find a deeper sense of stability when I rejoice in Your works? Cause me to remember it today, Lord: adoration of Christ comforts much anxiousness.

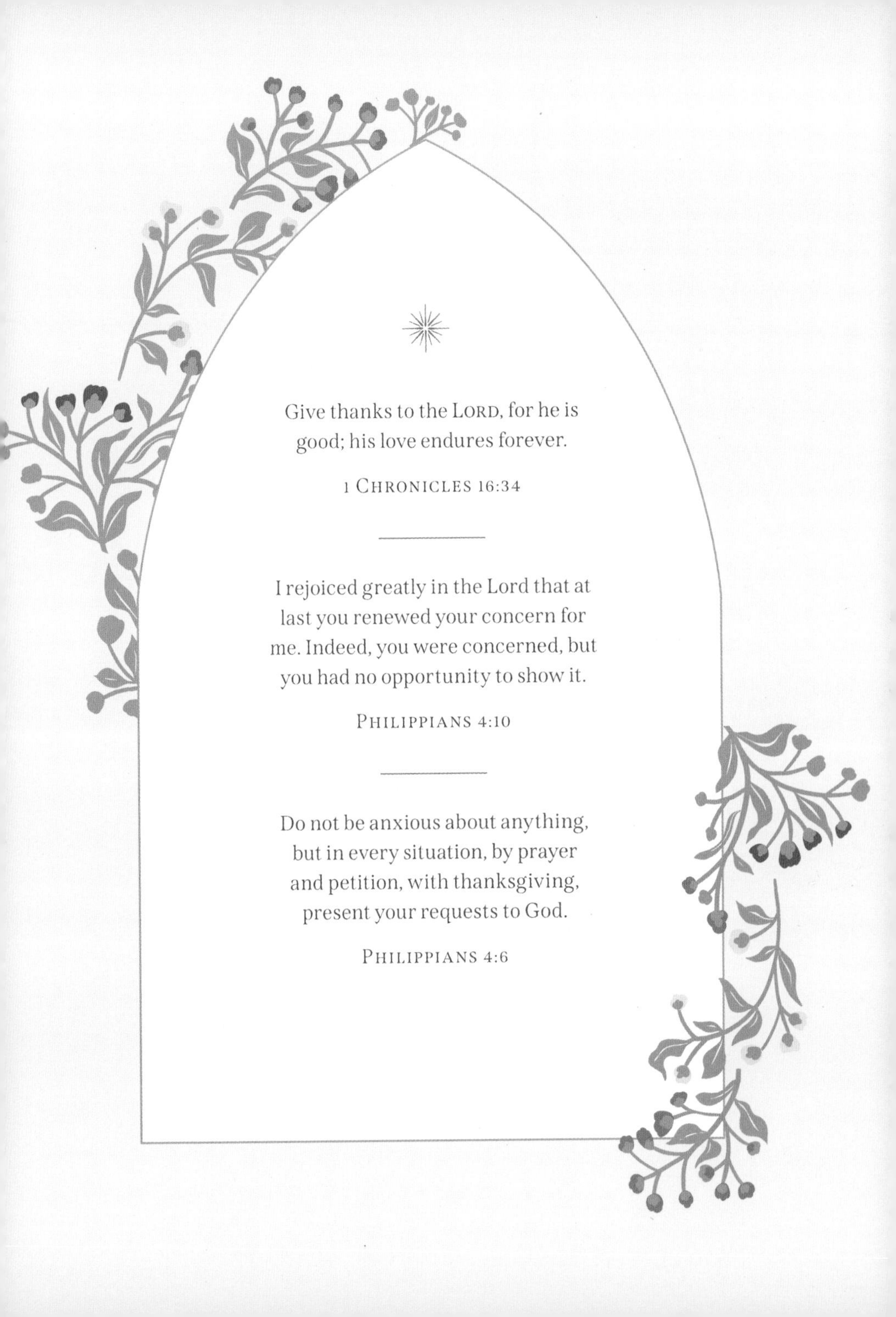

Give thanks to the LORD, for he is good; his love endures forever.

1 CHRONICLES 16:34

I rejoiced greatly in the Lord that at last you renewed your concern for me. Indeed, you were concerned, but you had no opportunity to show it.

PHILIPPIANS 4:10

Do not be anxious about anything, but in every situation, by prayer and petition, with thanksgiving, present your requests to God.

PHILIPPIANS 4:6

Gifts & Gratitudes

JANUARY

#

#

#

FEBRUARY

#

#

#

MARCH

#

#

#

APRIL

#

#

#

MAY

#

#

#

JUNE

#

#

#

6TH

JULY

#

#

#

AUGUST

#

#

#

SEPTEMBER

#

#

#

OCTOBER

#

#

#

NOVEMBER

#

#

#

DECEMBER

#

#

#

The LORD is my strength and shield. I trust him with all my heart. He helps me, and my heart is filled with joy. I burst out in songs of thanksgiving.

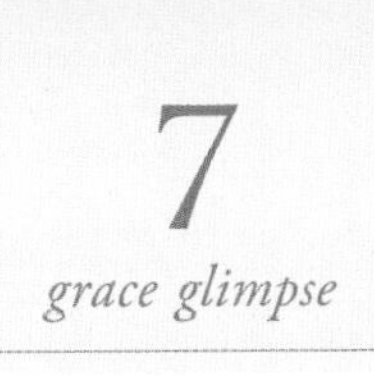

7

grace glimpse

Trusting Grace

He who did not spare his own Son, but gave him up for us all—how will he not also, along with him, graciously give us all things?

ROMANS 8:32

Worry can be my natural posture—the way I curl my toes up; how I angle my jaw, braced, brows chiseled with lines of distrust; how I don't fold my hands in prayer, but rather weld them into tight fists of control.

Worry can be the facade of taking action when prayer really is. And when I express that I'm *stressed*, is it really my attempt to prove how indispensable I am? Or does disguising my deep fears and worries as *stress* seem braver somehow?

Trust is the antithesis of stress. An untroubled heart relaxes, trusts, leans assured into His ever-dependable arms. "Oh, the joys of those who trust the LORD" (Psalm 40:4 NLT). But how to learn trust like that?

I can't fill with joy until I learn how to trust: "May the God of hope fill you with all *joy* and peace as you *trust* in him, so that you may overflow" (Romans 15:13, emphasis added). The full life, the one that authentically sits fully with all the nuanced and complicated emotions of life, and still makes space for joy and peace, happens only as the soul comes to more fully trust.

And—if trust must be earned, hasn't God unequivocally earned all our trust with the cross's bark on the raw wounds, the thorns pressed into the brow, your very name on His cracked lips? How will He not also graciously give us all things He sovereignly deems best and right? He's already given the incomprehensible—all of Himself. There is deep heartache in this busted and broken world, and still, there's more good beyond just this world: if He's given us the greatest and truest good of Himself—is there any *eternal* good we need that a good God would withhold?

Ultimately, the counting of all blessings is summed up in One: Christ, our Crossbeam, who is the beam who holds us and all things, together.

It's all Christ. Every moment, every event, every happening.

It's all in Christ, and in Christ we are always eternally soul-safe.

Lord, cause me to take a deep breath right now and really trust in my Savior—that He truly saves. Thank You, Lord; in my Savior I am always soul-safe.

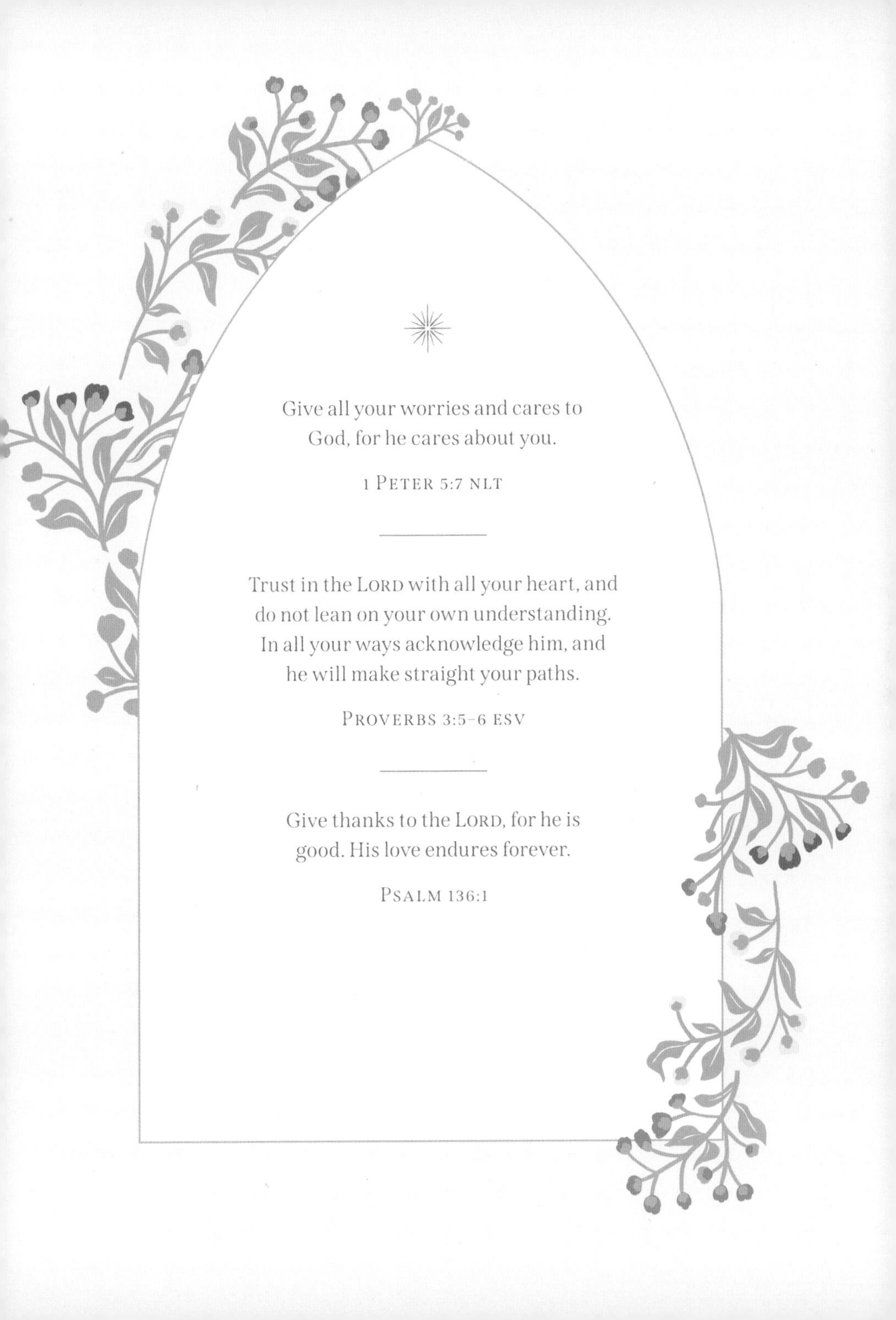

Give all your worries and cares to
God, for he cares about you.

1 PETER 5:7 NLT

Trust in the LORD with all your heart, and
do not lean on your own understanding.
In all your ways acknowledge him, and
he will make straight your paths.

PROVERBS 3:5–6 ESV

Give thanks to the LORD, for he is
good. His love endures forever.

PSALM 136:1

Gifts & Gratitudes

JANUARY

#

#

#

FEBRUARY

#

#

#

MARCH

#

#

#

APRIL

#

#

#

MAY

#

#

#

JUNE

#

#

#

7TH

JULY

#
#
#

AUGUST

#
#
#

SEPTEMBER

#
#
#

OCTOBER

#
#
#

NOVEMBER

#
#
#

DECEMBER

#
#
#

There is a time for everything, and a season for every activity under the heavens . . . a time to weep and a time to laugh, a time to mourn and a time to dance.

ECCLESIASTES 3:1, 4

8

grace glimpse

Slowing Grace

As a father has compassion on his children, so the Lord has compassion on those who fear him; for he knows how we are formed, he remembers that we are dust.

Psalm 103:13–14

God gives us time. But how do we make time for the God who gives us time, every single moment? A well-known pastor, and wise mentor of mine, was once asked what his most profound regret in life was: "Being in a hurry."

He explained:

> Getting to the next thing without fully entering the thing in front of me. I cannot think of a single advantage I've ever gained from being in a hurry.

> But a thousand broken and missed things, tens of thousands, lie in the wake of all the rushing. . . . Through all that haste, I thought I was *making up time*. It turns out I was *throwing it away*.[1]

Is it possible that in our rushing, we break our own lives?

Haste makes waste. All our hurry makes us hurt, and hurry always empties a soul. Who actually knows how to take time and live with soul and body and God all in sync?

The reality is: life is so urgent it necessitates living slow.

In Christ, the most urgent necessitates a slow and steady reverence. In Christ, time is not running out. In Christ, we fill, gaining time. We stand on the brink of eternity. So there is enough time.

Time to breathe deeply. Time to laugh long. Time to give God glory and to rest deeply and to sing joy defiantly and surely, even now. And there is the daily grace of just enough time in a day not to feel hounded, or pressed, or driven, or wild to get it all done. There is time to grab the jacket off the hook and time to go out into the air and sky and green. And time to read and exhale and wonder and give thanks—because there is more than enough time when we take up residence in the presence of the God over time, who is carrying us into forever beyond time.

Lord, I can't fully express my gratitude for the time You've given, all a gift.

I want to slow down and spend my life really living today, really experiencing the gifts in all these grace moments.

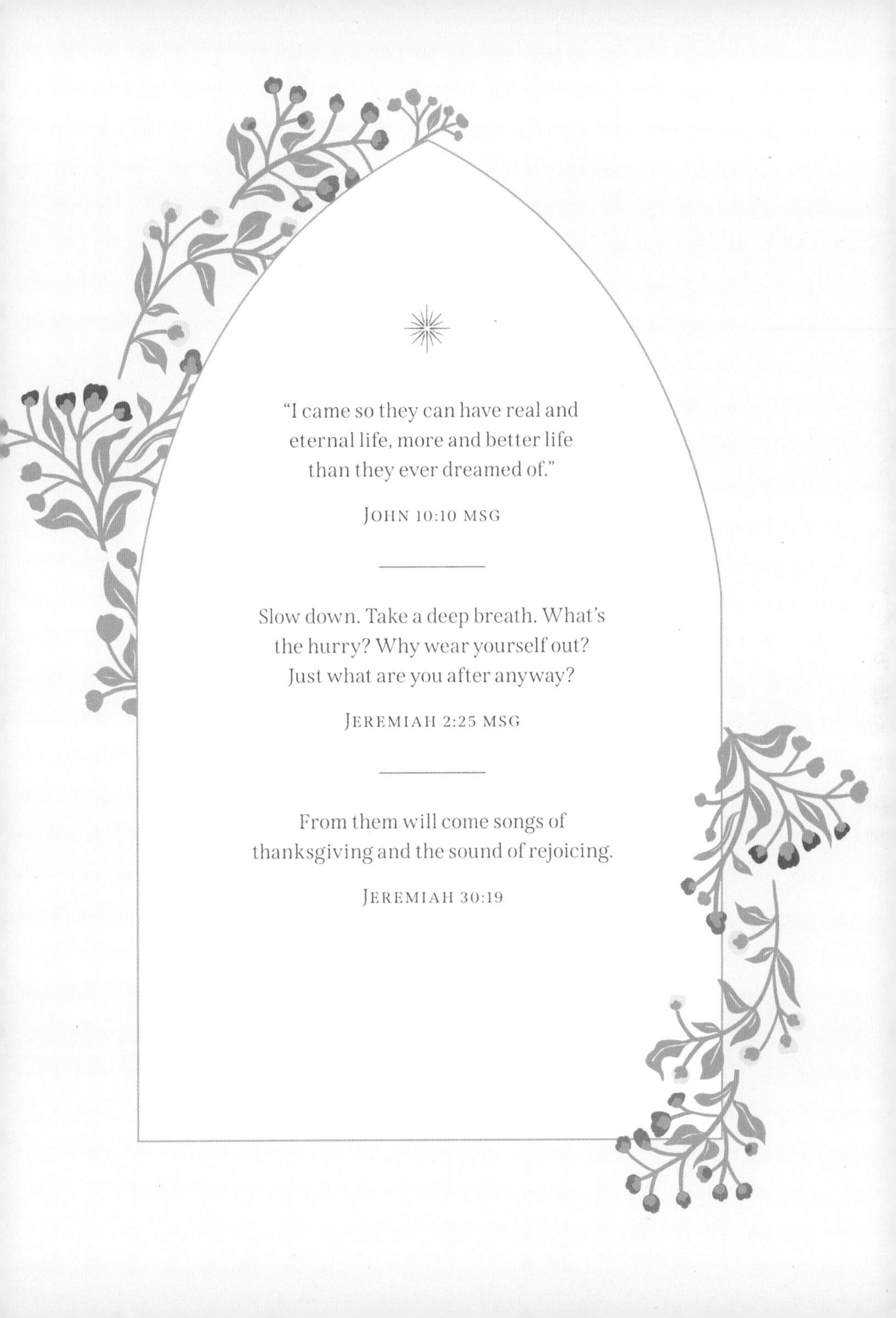

"I came so they can have real and eternal life, more and better life than they ever dreamed of."

John 10:10 MSG

Slow down. Take a deep breath. What's the hurry? Why wear yourself out? Just what are you after anyway?

Jeremiah 2:25 MSG

From them will come songs of thanksgiving and the sound of rejoicing.

Jeremiah 30:19

Gifts & Gratitudes

JANUARY

#

#

#

FEBRUARY

#

#

#

MARCH

#

#

#

APRIL

#

#

#

MAY

#

#

#

JUNE

#

#

#

8TH

JULY

#

#

#

AUGUST

#

#

#

SEPTEMBER

#

#

#

OCTOBER

#

#

#

NOVEMBER

#

#

#

DECEMBER

#

#

#

The peace of God, which transcends all understanding, will guard your hearts and your minds in Christ Jesus.

PHILIPPIANS 4:7 ESV

9

grace glimpse

Present Grace

The heavens are the work of your hands. . . . Like clothing you will change them and they will be discarded. But you remain the same, and your years will never end. The children of your servants will live in your presence.

PSALM 102:25–28

It's strange how the mind works.

The mind would rather fret about the future or pine over the past—so the mind can keep clinging to its own illusion of control. But time, this current moment? It cannot be controlled. And what a mind can't control, it tends to discount, brush past.

It's the battle plan of the enemy of the soul—to keep us blind to this current moment, the one we can't control, to keep us blind to Him, the One who controls everything.

What if instead of discounting the current moment, the uncontrollable, the simply given, we counted on it—and on the God who controls it all?

What if all our running around is only our trying to run away from God—the great I AM, present in the present moment?

What if we woke to now and refused to hurry, because we didn't want to refuse God?

It is the present moment alone that holds the possibility of coming into the presence of God.

Look around, breathe deeply, trust . . . and enter into this one moment.

Now could be an altar. *This time* could be a tabernacle.

In God, there is no time, only eternity—or more simply, only now. His name is I AM.

Here—*wherever your feet are*—is where you can love Him.

Lord God, forgive all the running around that is merely a running away from You. Today, cause me to refuse to hurry because I don't want to refuse You. This present moment holds the possibility of coming into Your presence.

Look carefully then how you walk,
not as unwise but as wise, making
the best use of the time.

EPHESIANS 5:15-16 ESV

I will give thanks to you, LORD,
with all my heart; I will tell of
all your wonderful deeds.

PSALM 9:1

You make known to me the path of life; in
your presence there is fullness of joy; at
your right hand are pleasures forevermore.

PSALM 16:11 ESV

Gifts & Gratitudes

JANUARY

\# ______ ______________________

\# ______ ______________________

\# ______ ______________________

FEBRUARY

\# ______ ______________________

\# ______ ______________________

\# ______ ______________________

MARCH

\# ______ ______________________

\# ______ ______________________

\# ______ ______________________

APRIL

\# ______ ______________________

\# ______ ______________________

\# ______ ______________________

MAY

\# ______ ______________________

\# ______ ______________________

\# ______ ______________________

JUNE

\# ______ ______________________

\# ______ ______________________

\# ______ ______________________

9TH

JULY

#

#

#

AUGUST

#

#

#

SEPTEMBER

#

#

#

OCTOBER

#

#

#

NOVEMBER

#

#

#

DECEMBER

#

#

#

"Give your entire attention to what God is doing right now, and don't get worked up about what may or may not happen tomorrow. God will help you deal with whatever hard things come up when the time comes."

Matthew 6:34 msg

10

grace glimpse

Recognizing Grace

What I mean, brothers and sisters, is that the time is short . . . for this world in its present form is passing away.

1 CORINTHIANS 7:29, 31

Who has time for all this *more* life brings us—more pressures, more problems, more challenges, more mess, more stress? All kinds of things can unexpectedly enter into your day, only to leave you all out of sorts.

The pulse can quicken in these moments and wise thinking can slow down in the pummeling of it all.

And this notion of entering fully into the moment can actually feel overwhelming, like stepping into a river running wild.

Yet there is a way through every day to the promised land of more of His presence.

And there's a way to preach the way through to the soul:
Calm.
Haste makes waste.
Remember:

- *Life is not an emergency. Life is brief and it is fleeting, but it is not an emergency.*
- *Emergencies are sudden, unexpected events–but is anything under the sun unexpected to God?*
- *Stay calm, fully enter into what is grace even in this moment, and give thanks.*
- *There is always a way to give thanks for at least something because an all-good, all-powerful God has all these things–all things–always under control.*

And so I preach to myself to hold it mindfully, attentively . . . thankfully:
Life is not an emergency–but a gift.

Father, with all the gifts I count, You are filling me, giving me more time to recognize the significance of the story You are writing on these days. Cause me to slow down today and truly taste of Your very real goodness, even here . . . especially in Yourself.

Always giving thanks to God
the Father for everything, in the
name of our Lord Jesus Christ.

EPHESIANS 5:20

Forget the former things; do not dwell on
the past. See, I am doing a new thing!

ISAIAH 43:18–19

Therefore, if anyone is in Christ,
the new creation has come: The
old has gone, the new is here!

2 CORINTHIANS 5:17

Gifts & Gratitudes

JANUARY

____________ ____

____________ ____

____________ ____

FEBRUARY

____________ ____

____________ ____

____________ ____

MARCH

____________ ____

____________ ____

____________ ____

APRIL

____________ ____

____________ ____

____________ ____

MAY

____________ ____

____________ ____

____________ ____

JUNE

____________ ____

____________ ____

____________ ____

10TH

JULY

#

#

#

AUGUST

#

#

#

SEPTEMBER

#

#

#

OCTOBER

#

#

#

NOVEMBER

#

#

#

DECEMBER

#

#

#

I will praise God's name in song and
glorify him with thanksgiving.

PSALM 69:30

Singing Grace

Always giving thanks for all things in the name of our Lord Jesus Christ.

EPHESIANS 5:20 NASB

In early spring, the frogs return, the frogs and their song.

Why does the trilling in the throat of a frog do this wondrous thing inside of me?

A symphony of sound, trilling low and deep, fills the spaces between the trees, lifts us too. With everyday eyes, I can't see the singers at all. It takes time for eyes to adjust to stillness, and only the slow really see.

Then—there they are, I can see the frogs there on the far side of the pond. *There,* these glinting eyes flickering up through waters! The peepers are back, and, staying so still, we can see them. We can see the source of the song. Who doesn't want front-row seats to glory?

Could we pick our way across the swamp to get any closer to them and this symphony of spring?

Our middle daughter and I swish-swash farther out, as far as we can go. Then sit and wait.

We say nothing, she and I, but we watch the swamp's mirror, waiting stock-still for the singers to surface. We wait. Then one by one, they pop to the light. We catch our breath—dare not move.

And tentatively it comes, this chorus, then a crescendo, throaty yet gilded, and she squeezes my hand and we're spellbound, smiling silly, enthralled by spring's song.

I could sit here forever, listening. Long, so very long, we sit and soak in frog songs on golden pond.

When our toes are cold and the shadows stretch, I stand slow, not wanting to go.

"We leaving the frogs now?" she whispers up to me.

I nod, reluctant, and scoop up one wide-eyed little girl and whisper to us both the surprising ways of God:

"You can only hear your life sing—when you still."

Father God, You invite me to still. For the very best of reasons. So today, I will. I've been missing the songs of Your glory far too long.

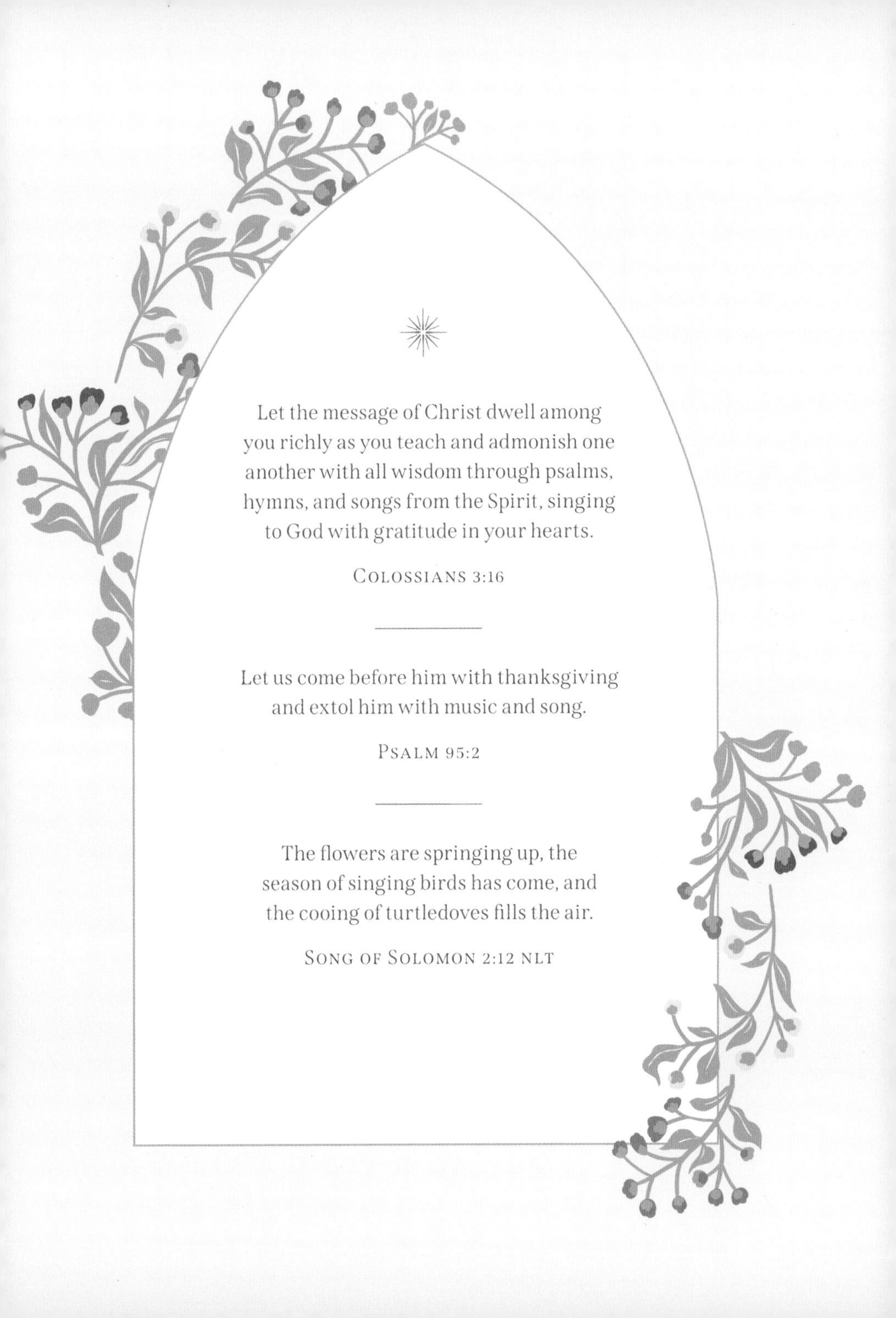

Let the message of Christ dwell among you richly as you teach and admonish one another with all wisdom through psalms, hymns, and songs from the Spirit, singing to God with gratitude in your hearts.

Colossians 3:16

Let us come before him with thanksgiving and extol him with music and song.

Psalm 95:2

The flowers are springing up, the season of singing birds has come, and the cooing of turtledoves fills the air.

Song of Solomon 2:12 NLT

Gifts & Gratitudes

JANUARY

#

#

#

FEBRUARY

#

#

#

MARCH

#

#

#

APRIL

#

#

#

MAY

#

#

#

JUNE

#

#

#

11TH

JULY

#

#

#

AUGUST

#

#

#

SEPTEMBER

#

#

#

OCTOBER

#

#

#

NOVEMBER

#

#

#

DECEMBER

#

#

#

Draw near to God, and he will draw near to you.

JAMES 4:8 ESV

12

grace glimpse

Ugly Grace

For God was pleased to have all his fullness dwell in him, and through him to reconcile to himself all things.

COLOSSIANS 1:19–20

In German, it's *hübsch-hässlich.*

In French, *d'un beau affreux.*

Or it's what the impressionist painter Paul Gauguin encapsulated as *"Le laid peut être beau"*—the ugly can be beautiful.

The *ugly-beautiful.*

I wonder if maybe in the upside-down kingdom of God, what we regard as unlovely is, in Jesus, lovely. Because somewhere, underneath the grime of this broken world, everything has the radiant fingerprints of God on it. Seeing the world with Jesus' eyes, there's this unexpected opportunity to daily love the complicated unlovely into loveliness.

And, funny thing, when I draw the lens of my perspective up close to the ugly in my life, I see ways it might be beautiful too.

When I deeply see:

- bedsheets painted with highlighter? *Children live here!*
- dead rose left too long in vase? *Lingering memories of a brother's gift.*
- great-grandma's wicker laundry basket overflowing in the mudroom? *We had a full, rich weekend!*
- souvenirs left behind in the vehicle—a collection of shoes, Sunday school paper, Lego pieces? *We'll gather them up too.*
- dining room table spread out with thoughts and ideas? *We're thinking now.*
- pile of tossed shoes at the back door? *Worn memories of full days.*
- stack of tattered books? *Stories that have become us, that we now carry.*

What if all these things that could kinda be deemed ugly, non-aesthetic things, in their own way, are part of the gift list too?

God is always good and we are always loved . . . even when life doesn't look the way we imagined.

What if looking for the lovely in the ugly-beautiful is a way that makes life more meaningful?

Lord, draw me nearer to the messy situations in my life, the scarred places. Hold me close enough to You to see Your beauty through them.

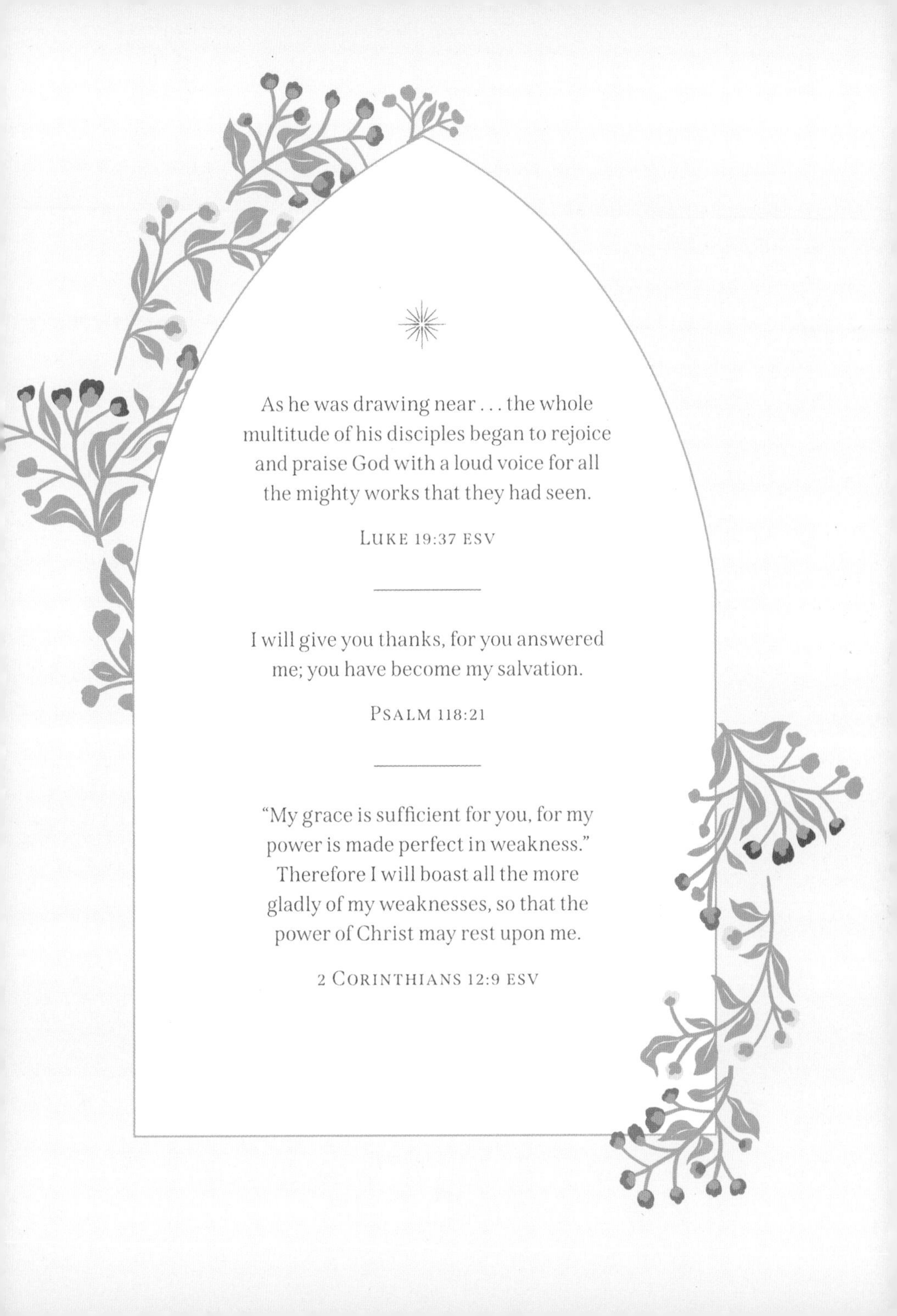

As he was drawing near . . . the whole multitude of his disciples began to rejoice and praise God with a loud voice for all the mighty works that they had seen.

LUKE 19:37 ESV

I will give you thanks, for you answered me; you have become my salvation.

PSALM 118:21

"My grace is sufficient for you, for my power is made perfect in weakness." Therefore I will boast all the more gladly of my weaknesses, so that the power of Christ may rest upon me.

2 CORINTHIANS 12:9 ESV

Gifts & Gratitudes

JANUARY

#

#

#

FEBRUARY

#

#

#

MARCH

#

#

#

APRIL

#

#

#

MAY

#

#

#

JUNE

#

#

#

12TH

JULY

#

#

#

AUGUST

#

#

#

SEPTEMBER

#

#

#

OCTOBER

#

#

#

NOVEMBER

#

#

#

DECEMBER

#

#

#

I do not treat the grace of God as meaningless.

GALATIANS 2:21 NLT

Graffiti Grace

Fear not, for I have redeemed you; I have called you by name, you are mine. . . . Because you are precious in my eyes, and honored, and I love you, I give men in return for you, peoples in exchange for your life.

ISAIAH 43:1, 4 ESV

Some days it's hard to make sense of all the tender things.

A friend—one who knew me back in the permed days of teased bangs in high school—and I go for a walk. She has questions of her own, and I nod and we try to give each other the gift of presence, the gift of witness and witness in a hurting world.

We're walking down a side street in town together, when I stop and reach for my camera. I aim the camera at the sidewalk, and my friend stops mid-sentence. She reads the words chalked on asphalt out loud, reads them slowly, like a decoding of everything.

"Hey beautiful, you are loved," is scrawled right there in bright white chalk on the sidewalk.

"Oh." She says it like an awakening. "And here I just thought it was graffiti."

I nod in the middle of my own epiphany.

What looks like graffiti can be grace.

All the writing on the wall could hold unlikely love notes.

"Kinda deciphers everything, doesn't it?" I say it to myself, only half asking. The other half of me is knowing with a certainty I've not felt before, and that's what jolts me, right there on the sidewalk: Grace isn't a mere Pollyanna feeling. It's a powerful force that reorients. Grace is the power of God, pulsating with this passionate love of God, this jolting, blazing, dangerous love that pierces all the dark with brilliant light—with brilliant love.

Grace is always coming to find you. Grace is always coming to wrap you up in the most beautiful love.

It's what everyone groping around, lost in the dark, and looking for answers, has to know: turn to see all kinds of grace upon grace, and you turn on all the lights.

Love always rightly deciphers everything.

Lord God, there will be walls I run into today, walls that seem to box me in, walls that have writing on them that I long to decode. When I rightly read Your Word, I can rightly read the world: the graffiti of this world is loving grace in Your hands.

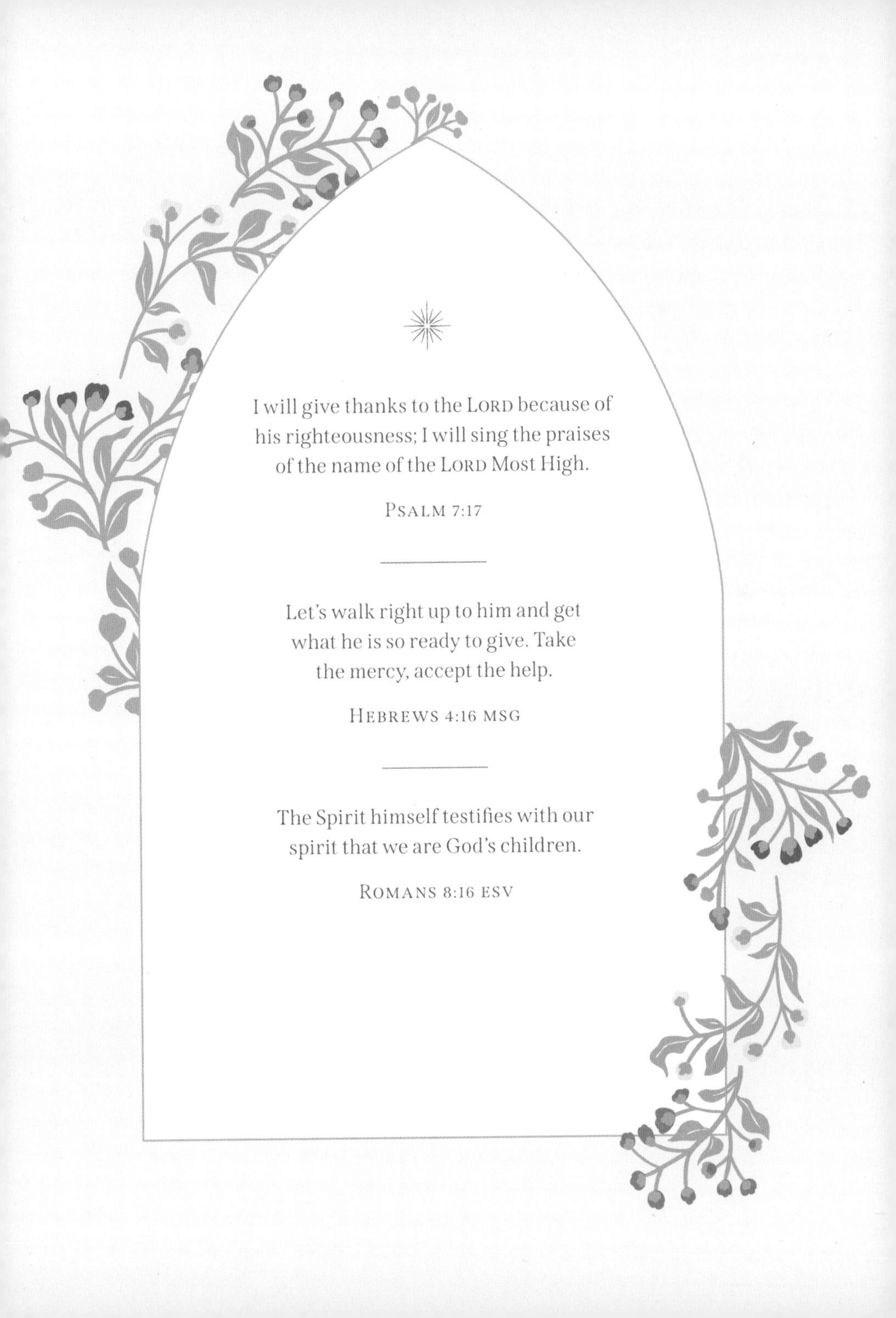

I will give thanks to the LORD because of his righteousness; I will sing the praises of the name of the LORD Most High.

PSALM 7:17

Let's walk right up to him and get what he is so ready to give. Take the mercy, accept the help.

HEBREWS 4:16 MSG

The Spirit himself testifies with our spirit that we are God's children.

ROMANS 8:16 ESV

Gifts & Gratitudes

JANUARY

#

#

#

FEBRUARY

#

#

#

MARCH

#

#

#

APRIL

#

#

#

MAY

#

#

#

JUNE

#

#

#

13TH

JULY

#

#

#

AUGUST

#

#

#

SEPTEMBER

#

#

#

OCTOBER

#

#

#

NOVEMBER

#

#

#

DECEMBER

#

#

#

May the God of hope fill you with all joy and peace as you trust in him, so that you may overflow with hope by the power of the Holy Spirit.

ROMANS 15:13

14

grace glimpse

Coded Grace

I have learned how to be content with whatever I have. I know how to live on almost nothing or with everything. I have learned the secret of living in every situation, whether it is with a full stomach or empty, with plenty or little.

PHILIPPIANS 4:11–12 NLT

Sitting there before the window, I confess, I felt a bit struck. All these years, I had said my yes to God, but I wondered if there were ways I was really living more of a no to God.

To really fully live—at all—I needed to *know*, deep in my bones, how to live *eucharisteo,* that Greek word that means thanksgiving, *to give thanks*, but it is more all-encompassing than that: it is gratitude, born of grace, which gives rise to real joy.

So I had begun the list. Not of gifts I wanted, but of gifts I *already had*. That was the beginning, and I'd smiled, I can't believe how I had smiled.

Writing the list, it makes me feel . . . *happy. All day.* I can hardly believe how it does that, and I add one more gift to the list. *Swaths of sunlight across our old floors . . . dish soap bubbles in the sink, catching light . . . the creak of the door when he comes in.*

This thanks that I am writing, it seems so . . . small . . . trivial? But perhaps the "full of grace" vocabulary begins haltingly, simply, like a child, thankful for the childlike.

Doesn't the kingdom of heaven belong to all those with childlike wonder, childlike faith?

At first, it's this dare to count one thousand gifts, one thousand blessings, that keeps me going. That, and how happy it makes me—kinda giddy—this list-writing of all that is good and pure and lovely and beautiful. But what keeps me going is what I read in that Bible.

Twice Paul whispered it: "I have learned" (Philippians 4:11–12 NLT). Learned. I would have to learn *eucharisteo.* You need to learn it to live fully. Learn how to be thankful, whether empty or full. There it is—the secret to living joy in every situation is the full life of *eucharisteo.*

I'm ready for the hunt of gifts, the long sleuth for the good, the careful piecing together of all the grace upon grace. I'm ready to learn how to be grateful and happy, whether hands full or hands empty. *That is a secret worth spending a life on learning.*

I wake the next morning and I grip my pen, ink, to crack the code to joy.

God, so many days have dialects I don't understand. How in the world do I learn the language of joy? One can only crack the code of contentment by learning the language of Your love. Let me count the ways.

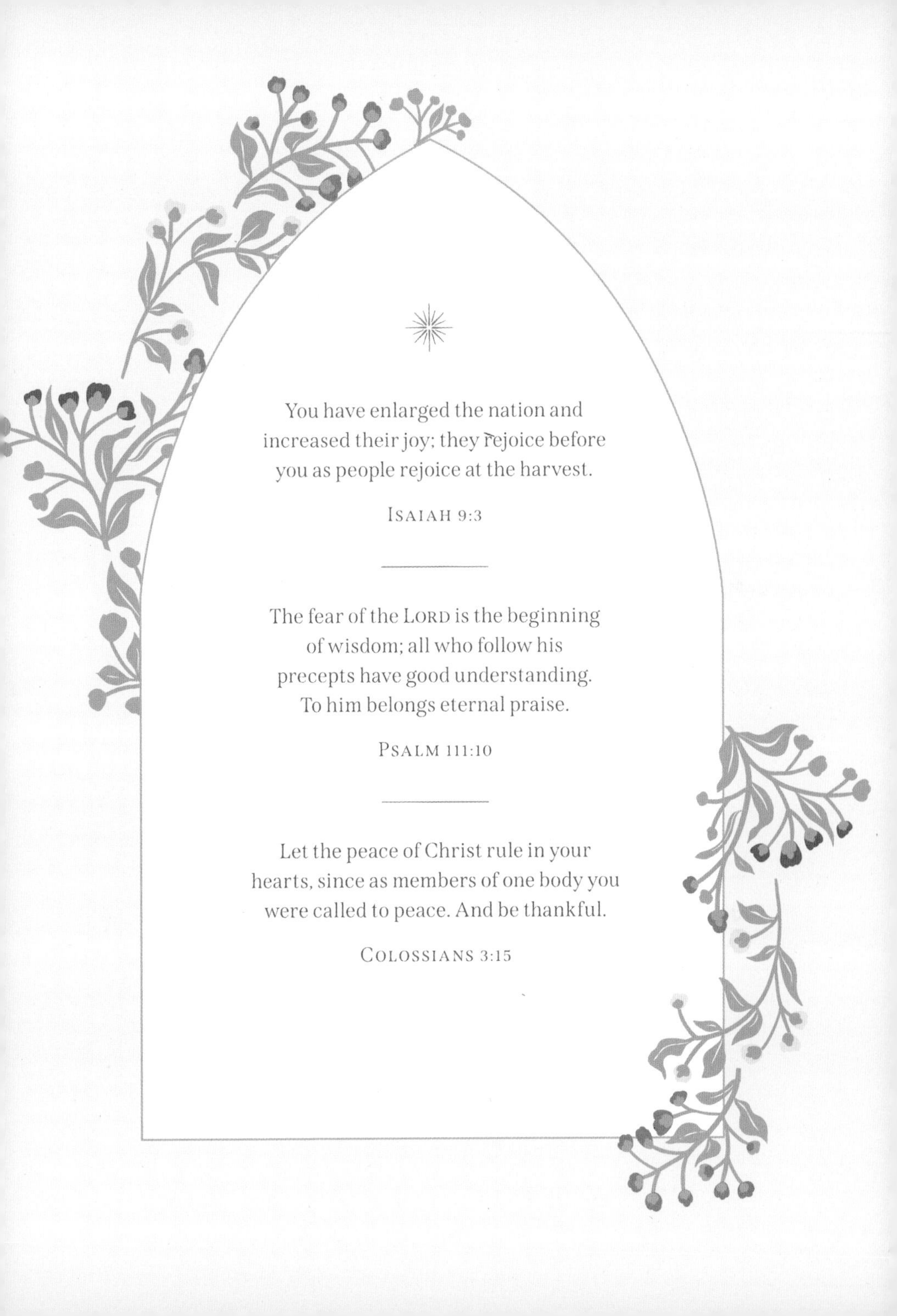

You have enlarged the nation and increased their joy; they rejoice before you as people rejoice at the harvest.

Isaiah 9:3

The fear of the Lord is the beginning of wisdom; all who follow his precepts have good understanding. To him belongs eternal praise.

Psalm 111:10

Let the peace of Christ rule in your hearts, since as members of one body you were called to peace. And be thankful.

Colossians 3:15

Gifts & Gratitudes

JANUARY

#

#

#

FEBRUARY

#

#

#

MARCH

#

#

#

APRIL

#

#

#

MAY

#

#

#

JUNE

#

#

#

14TH

JULY

#

#

#

AUGUST

#

#

#

SEPTEMBER

#

#

#

OCTOBER

#

#

#

NOVEMBER

#

#

#

DECEMBER

#

#

#

A good name is more desirable than great riches;
to be esteemed is better than silver or gold.

PROVERBS 22:1

15

grace glimpse

Naming Grace

He brought them to the man to see what he would name them; and whatever the man called each living creature, that was its name.

GENESIS 2:19–20

My list of naming God-gifts lies open on the counter: 117. Washing the warm eggs; 118. Crackle in fireplace; 119. Still-warm cookies.

And I am realizing, like a bit of an epiphany: naming is Edenic.

The first man's first task was to name. Adam completed creation with his Maker through the act of naming creatures. I am seeing it too: naming offers the gift of recognition. When I name moments—*thank You, Lord, for bedsheets in billowing winds, for fluff of sparrow landing on line, sun winter warm, and one last leaf still hanging in the orchard*—I discover my meaning and God's, and that to name gifts is to learn the language of paradise.

It's late one night, and in the lamplight when the bones finally rest, I read and turn a page and run unexpectedly into these words:

> Now, in the Bible a name . . . reveals the very essence of a thing, or rather its essence as God's gift. . . . To name a thing is to manifest the meaning and value God gave it, to know it as coming from God and to know its place and function within the cosmos created by God. To name a thing, in other words, is to bless God for it and in it.[1]

I read the words again. The heart palpitates hard with the wonder of it. All I can think is that my whim writing of one thousand gratitudes, the naming of the moments, this is truly a holy work *that is blessing God Himself.*

I read again: "To name a thing is to manifest the meaning and value God gave it."

In naming that which is right before me, that which I'd otherwise miss, the invisible becomes visible.

God is in the details; God is in the moment. God is in all that blurs by in a life—even hurts in a life.

And when you name the gifts in your life, you are blessing the very name of God Himself.

Lord, help me to name the graces You give me this day. Cause me to name the ways You love, so I can own my own name: Beloved.

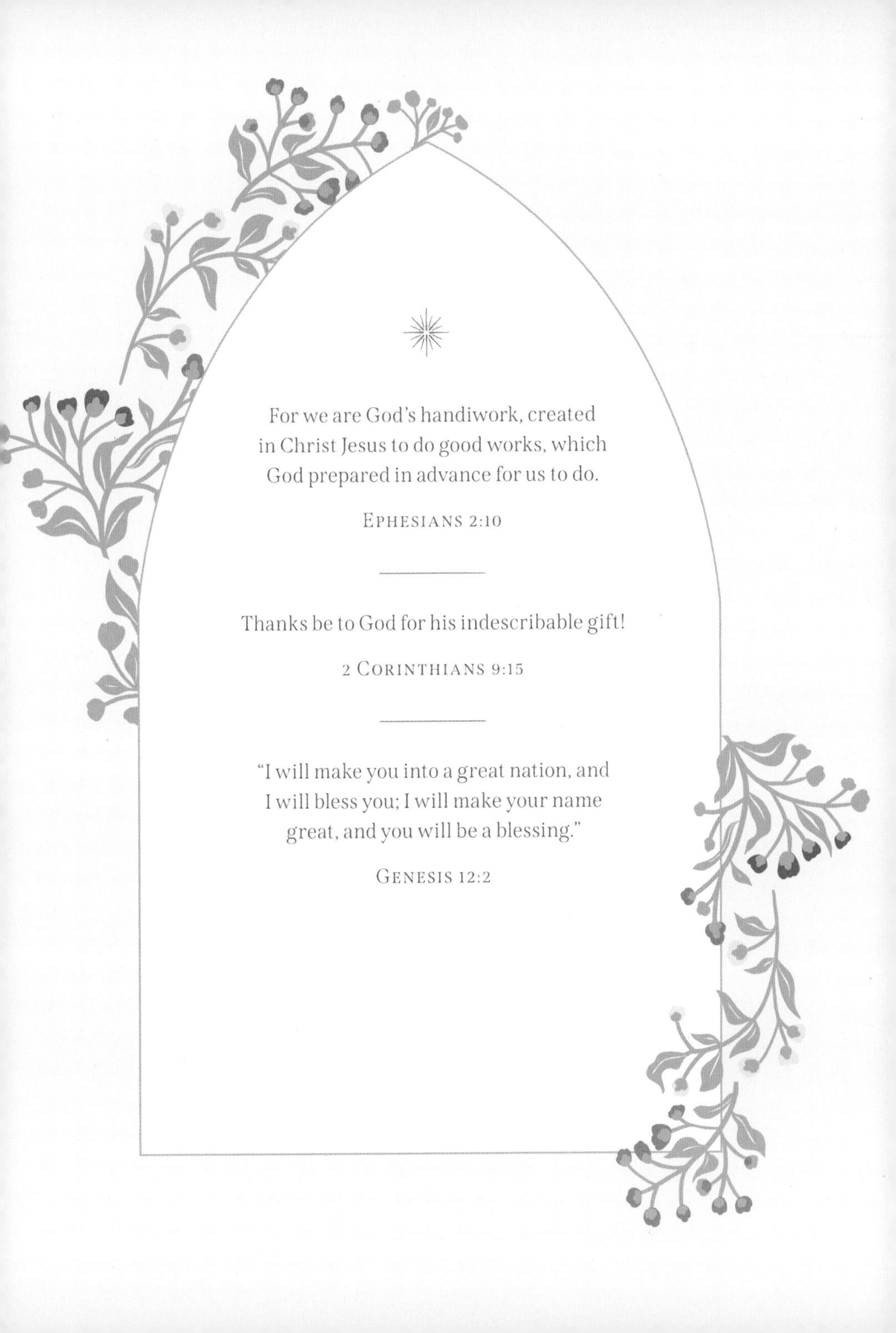

For we are God's handiwork, created in Christ Jesus to do good works, which God prepared in advance for us to do.

EPHESIANS 2:10

Thanks be to God for his indescribable gift!

2 CORINTHIANS 9:15

"I will make you into a great nation, and I will bless you; I will make your name great, and you will be a blessing."

GENESIS 12:2

Gifts & Gratitudes

JANUARY

____________ ____

____________ ____

____________ ____

FEBRUARY

____________ ____

____________ ____

____________ ____

MARCH

____________ ____

____________ ____

____________ ____

APRIL

____________ ____

____________ ____

____________ ____

MAY

____________ ____

____________ ____

____________ ____

JUNE

____________ ____

____________ ____

____________ ____

15TH

JULY

#

#

#

AUGUST

#

#

#

SEPTEMBER

#

#

#

OCTOBER

#

#

#

NOVEMBER

#

#

#

DECEMBER

#

#

#

Let me shout God's name with a praising song,
Let me tell his greatness in a prayer of thanks.

Psalm 69:30 msg

Praying Grace

I thank and praise you, God of my ancestors: You have given me wisdom and power.

DANIEL 2:23

It can be easy to be kind of fooled by the simplicity of *eucharisteo* and penning His love list. *Frogs. Sun. Journal. Love.*

Yet it's undeniable: It all feels startlingly hallowed, like you want to take your shoes off. God in the grace of all these gifts.

This is where Daniel, man of prayer, lived. You know, change agent Daniel, second-to-the-king Daniel, sleeping-in-perfect-peace-in-the-lions'-den Daniel. This was a man of power prayer—and the reason his prayers moved kings and lion jaws was because Daniel "got down on his knees and prayed, *giving thanks* to his God" (Daniel 6:10, emphasis added). Three times a day, what Daniel prayed were prayers of *thanksgiving*.

Prayer—*to be prayer*, to have any power to change anything—must first speak thanks: "In every situation, by prayer and petition, *with thanksgiving*, present your requests to God" (Philippians 4:6, emphasis added). "*First*, I tell you to pray for all people, asking God for what they need and *being thankful to him*" (1 Timothy 2:1 NCV, emphasis added). Prayer without ceasing is only possible in a life of continual thanks.

The gift list *is* thinking upon His goodness—and this, *this* pleases Him most! *And* this is what most profits my own soul. If clinging to His goodness is the highest form of prayer, then seeing His goodness with a pen, with a word of thanks, these really are the most sacred acts of our everyday life.

Daniel was only a man of prayer because he was a man of thanks, and the only way to be a person of prayer is to *be a person of thanks*. And more than sporadic, general thanks, but three times a day *eucharisteo, equals a life* of multiplied joy in the grace and goodness of God.

Lord, You are the Giver infinitely greater than the sum of all gifts, and how can I not slow and bow? Kneel in gratitude? Slow, wherever I am, in adoration? Could the miracle of becoming a person of prayer begin with just two words: "Thank You"?

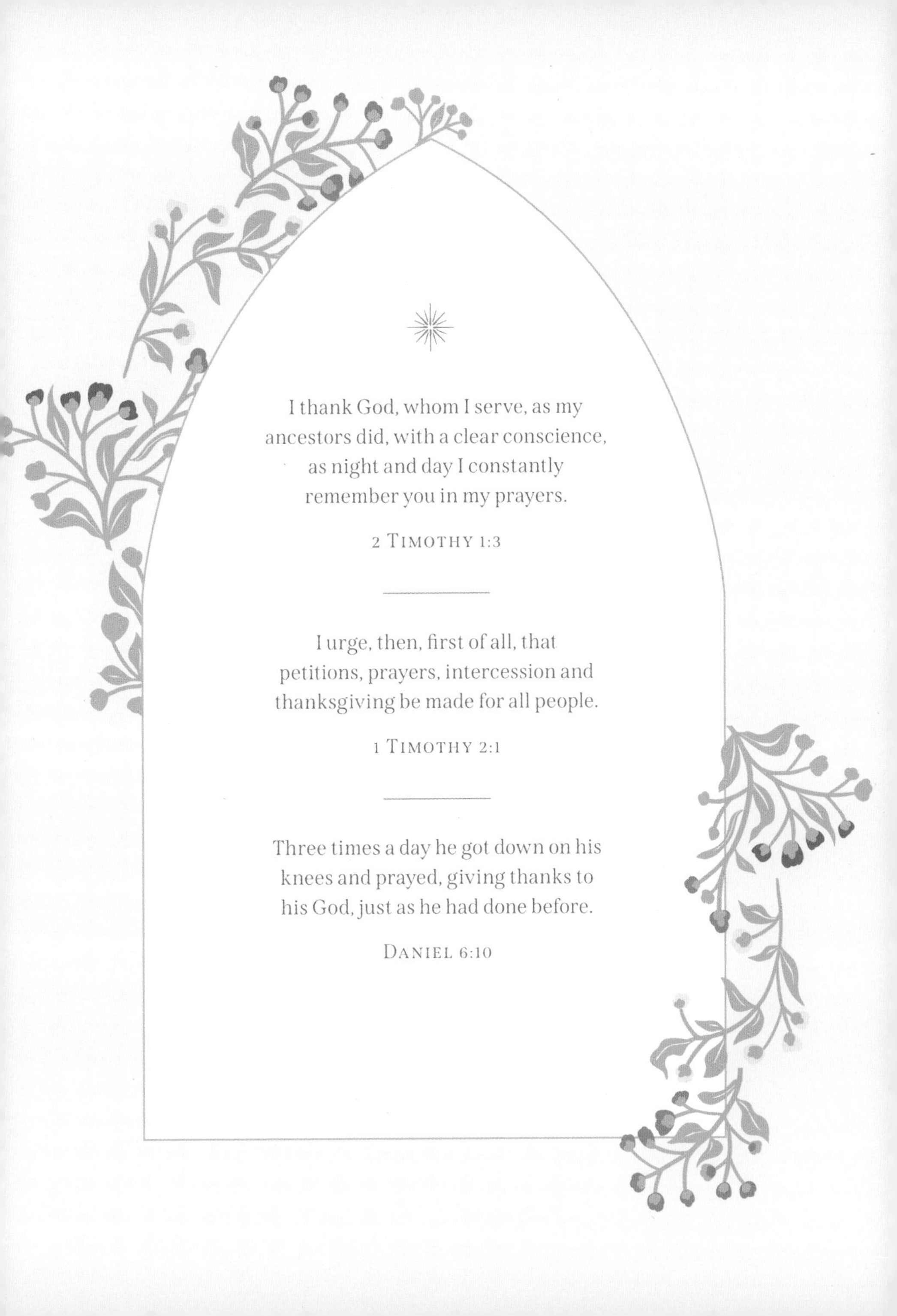

I thank God, whom I serve, as my ancestors did, with a clear conscience, as night and day I constantly remember you in my prayers.

2 TIMOTHY 1:3

I urge, then, first of all, that petitions, prayers, intercession and thanksgiving be made for all people.

1 TIMOTHY 2:1

Three times a day he got down on his knees and prayed, giving thanks to his God, just as he had done before.

DANIEL 6:10

Gifts & Gratitudes

JANUARY

#

#

#

FEBRUARY

#

#

#

MARCH

#

#

#

APRIL

#

#

#

MAY

#

#

#

JUNE

#

#

#

16TH

JULY

#

#

#

AUGUST

#

#

#

SEPTEMBER

#

#

#

OCTOBER

#

#

#

NOVEMBER

#

#

#

DECEMBER

#

#

#

And whatever you do, whether in word or deed,
do it all in the name of the Lord Jesus, giving
thanks to God the Father through him.

COLOSSIANS 3:17

17

grace glimpse

All-Here Grace

Sacrifice thank offerings to God, fulfill your vows to the Most High. . . .
Those who sacrifice thank offerings honor me.

Psalm 50:14, 23

With my hand still dribbling wet from dishes, I seize the pen and record another one, in that journal always lying out flat: *362. Suds . . . all color in sun.*

I lay down the pen, dry my hands on the dish towel, dab at water spots transfusing into ink.

The house is a bit of a mess.

And my tired heart speaks to the heart of God: I don't really want *more* time; I just want *enough* time, time to do my one life well.

I slip my palm under water and then raise my hand with the membrane of a life span of moments. In the light, the sheerness of bubble shimmers.

Bands of garnet, cobalt, flowing luminous. Wonder right there in the middle of the sink.

I see. I see through to the pattern. The way my life, vapor, is shaping. And I almost hadn't noticed.

Time is a relentless river.

It rages on, a respecter of no one.

And this is the only way to slow time down. When you fully enter time's swift current, into the current moment with the weight of all your attention, you slow the torrent of time down with the weight of you all here.

That's it: *the only way to slow down time is with the weight of all your attention.*

The bubble in my hand quivers, a rainbow at the fringes.

And blind eyes see: it's this for the glory of God everywhere that slows a life, *and time*, right down.

In this space of time and sphere, you can be attentive, aware, accepting the whole of the moment, weighing it down with you all here.

Full attention fills much emptiness.

Forgive me, Father, for not being all here. When Your very name is I AM and You are in the present and here is where I can love You. Today, when I race ahead–return me to all here.

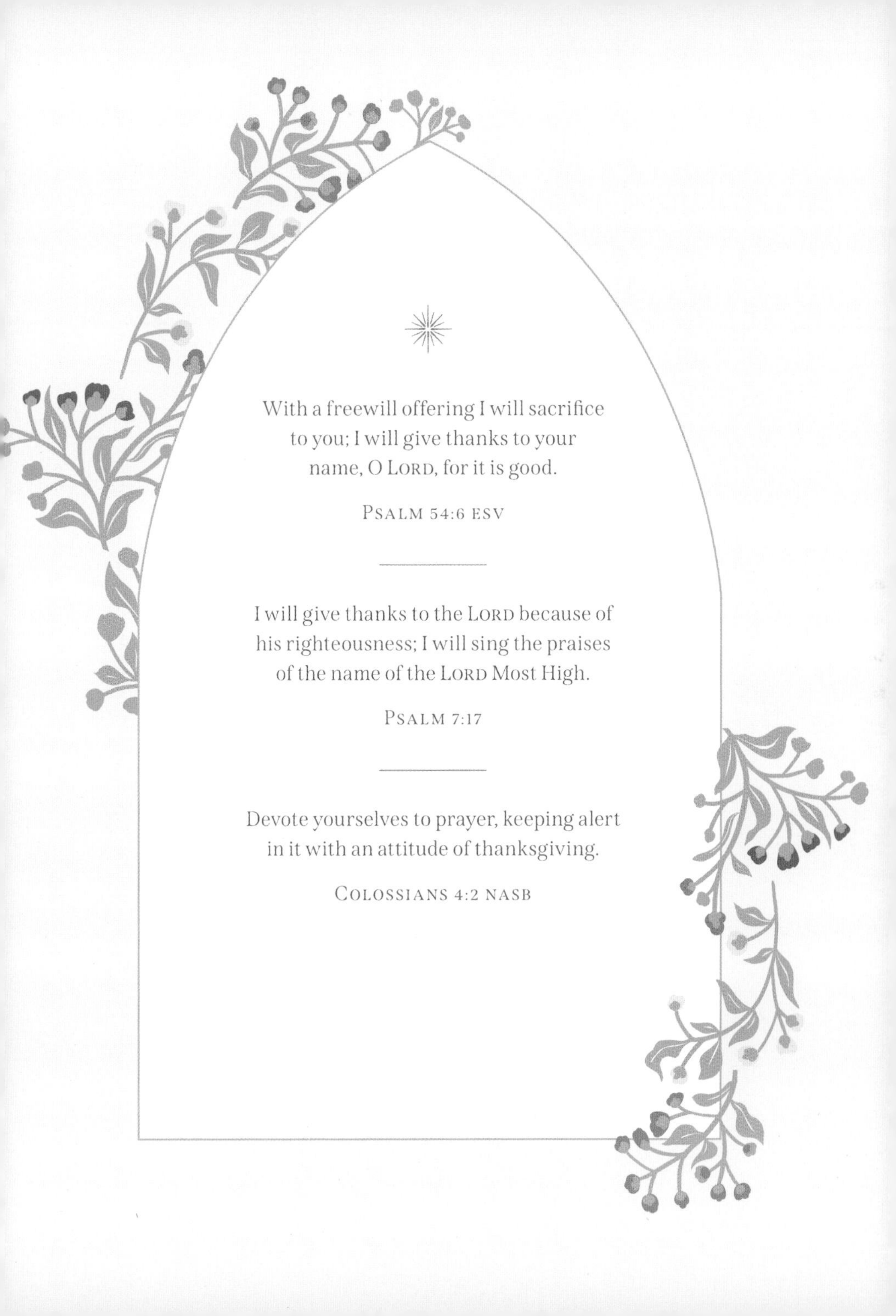

With a freewill offering I will sacrifice to you; I will give thanks to your name, O LORD, for it is good.

PSALM 54:6 ESV

I will give thanks to the LORD because of his righteousness; I will sing the praises of the name of the LORD Most High.

PSALM 7:17

Devote yourselves to prayer, keeping alert in it with an attitude of thanksgiving.

COLOSSIANS 4:2 NASB

Gifts & Gratitudes

JANUARY

#
#
#

FEBRUARY

#
#
#

MARCH

#
#
#

APRIL

#
#
#

MAY

#
#
#

JUNE

#
#
#

17TH

JULY

#

#

#

AUGUST

#

#

#

SEPTEMBER

#

#

#

OCTOBER

#

#

#

NOVEMBER

#

#

#

DECEMBER

#

#

#

Be strong and do not give up, for
your work will be rewarded.

2 CHRONICLES 15:7

18

grace glimpse

Hammering Grace

Seek and you will find; knock and the door will be opened to you. . . . Therefore everyone who hears these words of mine and puts them into practice is like a wise man who built his house on the rock.

MATTHEW 7:7, 24

A contemporary and admirer of Martin Luther, the theologian Erasmus, once said, "A nail is driven out by another nail; habit is overcome by habit."[1]

When I read this, I was surprised I hadn't known sooner, and I am sad for all that would have changed if only I had.

In this counting of one thousand gifts and graces and gratitudes, I discover that slapping a sloppy brush of thanksgiving over everything in my life leaves me deeply thankful for very few things in my life.

Life-changing gratitude does not fasten to a life unless nailed through with one very specific nail at a time.

Do not disdain the small. Little nails and a steady hammer can rebuild a life.

Eucharisteo precedes the miracle; thanksgiving precedes the miracle of more joy, more wonder, more awe, more gladness in God.

I look down at the pen. This pen—using this pen to write down gifts and gratitudes is nothing less than the driving of nails, nails driving out my habits of discontent and driving in my habit of *eucharisteo*. Because the habit of discontentment can only be driven out by hammering in one iron sharper: the sleek pin of gratitude.

I keep hammering.

And I pick up the journal. Paul had twice said he had to *learn*. And learning requires *practice*.

Is this why I had never fully learned the language of "thanks in all things"? Though pastors preached it, I still had come home . . . and griped on. I had never *practiced*.

Practice is the hardest part of learning, and training is the essence of transformation.

Practice, practice, practice. Hammer. Hammer. Hammer.

This training might prove to be the hardest of your life.

It just might save very real parts of your life.

Lord God, Your Son took the ringing of the hammer and the pounding of the nails to buy my salvation. I offer You up my open hands. Drive out the nails of habitual grumbling with the nails of habitual gratitude.

Whether you eat or drink, or whatever you do, do all to the glory of God.

1 CORINTHIANS 10:31 ESV

I lift up my eyes to the mountains—
where does my help come from?
My help comes from the LORD, the
Maker of heaven and earth.

PSALM 121:1–2

Then, by the will of God, I will be able to come to you with a joyful heart, and we will be an encouragement to each other.

ROMANS 15:32 NLT

Gifts & Gratitudes

JANUARY

______ ______________________

______ ______________________

______ ______________________

FEBRUARY

______ ______________________

______ ______________________

______ ______________________

MARCH

______ ______________________

______ ______________________

______ ______________________

APRIL

______ ______________________

______ ______________________

______ ______________________

MAY

______ ______________________

______ ______________________

______ ______________________

JUNE

______ ______________________

______ ______________________

______ ______________________

18TH

JULY

#

#

#

AUGUST

#

#

#

SEPTEMBER

#

#

#

OCTOBER

#

#

#

NOVEMBER

#

#

#

DECEMBER

#

#

#

That's why I tell stories: to create readiness, to nudge the people toward a welcome awakening.

MATTHEW 13:13 MSG

19

grace glimpse

Awakening Grace

Give thanks in all circumstances; for this is God's will for you in Christ Jesus.

1 THESSALONIANS 5:18

It wasn't till Shalom, our middle daughter, pulled these two wee kitties into her arms that I knew something in me had been kinda walking dead all day.

But the way those bundles of fur purred deep into the crook of her arm, so quiet? Something in me opened wide.

Shalom turned to look into the wide-eyed faces of these kitties, and she laughed, so in awe and full of life—and something stirred in me, so loud.

Maybe it was the way one of the tendrils of her hair fell that made me see that day—that I had fallen asleep much of the whole day to the glory of God right here.

You can miss much of your life when you miss the graces and gifts in your life that are right in front of you.

Who wants to live like this, and isn't that what Robert Louis Stevenson wrote?

"The man who forgets to be thankful has fallen asleep in life."[1]

You can forget to be thankful—*and really live*—in a thousand ways.

Shalom said it tickled, the way his tail flicked her nose. She said it, and her eyes, they laughed with all this light. But what was happening was she was tickling me awake.

The day's troubles fade as I live—as I give thanks—in the present moment.

When we fill the kitty dish, you can hear it, how they drink. Our girl lies right on her tummy so she can listen.

"Hear them, Mama?" Her eyes dance, she and I smiling over spilled milk, she and I waking up . . . lapping up life.

Giving thanks is an awakening to life—the breath of God upon the face, close and warm.

Father, Awakener of the dead, awaken me again today. Tendrils of Your grace will fall today—cause me not to forget to give thanks so I don't fall asleep to my life.

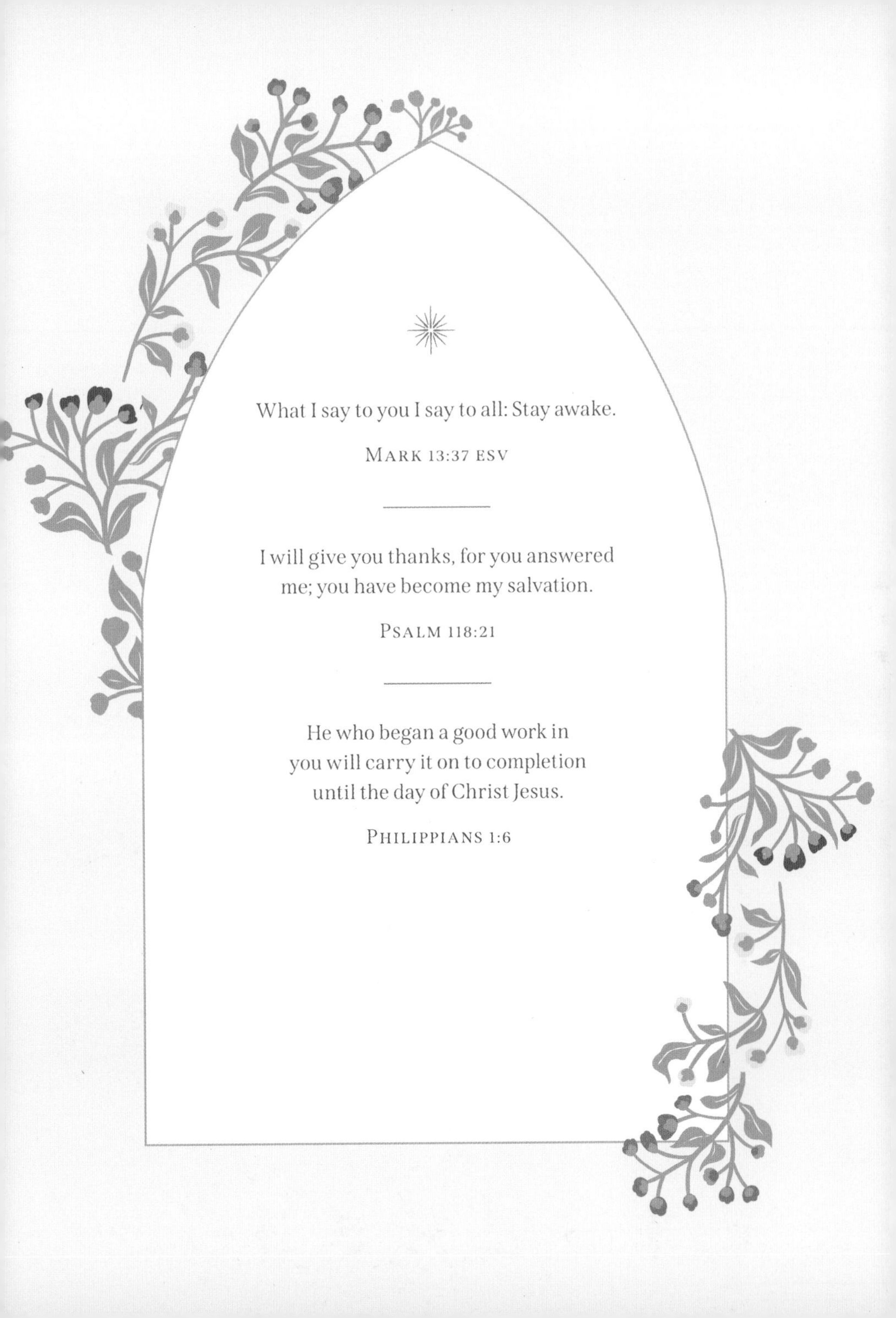

What I say to you I say to all: Stay awake.

MARK 13:37 ESV

I will give you thanks, for you answered me; you have become my salvation.

PSALM 118:21

He who began a good work in you will carry it on to completion until the day of Christ Jesus.

PHILIPPIANS 1:6

Gifts & Gratitudes

JANUARY

#

#

#

FEBRUARY

#

#

#

MARCH

#

#

#

APRIL

#

#

#

MAY

#

#

#

JUNE

#

#

#

19TH

JULY

#

#

#

AUGUST

#

#

#

SEPTEMBER

#

#

#

OCTOBER

#

#

#

NOVEMBER

#

#

#

DECEMBER

#

#

#

Whoever regards one day as special does so to the Lord.

ROMANS 14:6

20

grace glimpse

All-Is-Well Grace

Then God opened her eyes and she saw a well of water.

GENESIS 21:19

It's true: Hagar and her boy were dying of thirst with a well less than a bowshot away.

How do we find God in the mess? *Why is it so hard?*

Practice, practice.

What insanity compels me to shrivel up when there is joy's water to be had here? In everyday wilderness, I keep circling back to this: it's possible to be blind to joy's well and not realize *there's always a well somewhere here.*

If I am rejecting the joy that is hidden somewhere deep, even in this moment, in hard and tender stories, am I not somehow ultimately rejecting the grace and kindness of God right here?

If I don't look for the ways God cares, if I don't take time to notice the grace of God right here—how much do I want God?

The well is always here somewhere, because God is always here somehow—precisely because He does *care.* In His presence is fullness of joy. *He is here, right here, even in this tender moment.*

You have to be open to the possibility of even the smallest well existing here in this desert, before you can drink from it. You could be open to there being more than just parched wilderness right here.

> Thereafter, Hagar used another name to refer to the LORD, who had spoken to her. She said, "You are the God who sees me." She also said, "Have I truly seen the One who sees me?" So that well was named Beer-lahai-roi (which means "well of the Living One who sees me"). (Genesis 16:13–14 NLT)

It's easy to forget the One who sees you, but if you slow to see gifts and grace, you catch glimpses of God in painful deserts.

Live *eucharisteo* and you see a bit more clearly.

Cup hands and taste how more of the world is water.

The well, it is still here, God is still here.

There is always somehow, someway, a well—all is well.

Lord, that You would give one grace after another—tune my senses to see Your grace. Focus my sight to see the well—that, even now, all is well.

Fear not, for I *am* with you; be not dismayed, for I *am* your God. I will strengthen you, yes, I will help you, I will uphold you with My righteous right hand.

ISAIAH 41:10 NKJV

He even sees me in the dark! At night I'm immersed in the light!

PSALM 139:11 MSG

But thanks be to God! He gives us the victory through our Lord Jesus Christ.

1 CORINTHIANS 15:57

Gifts & Gratitudes

JANUARY

______ ____________________

______ ____________________

______ ____________________

FEBRUARY

______ ____________________

______ ____________________

______ ____________________

MARCH

______ ____________________

______ ____________________

______ ____________________

APRIL

______ ____________________

______ ____________________

______ ____________________

MAY

______ ____________________

______ ____________________

______ ____________________

JUNE

______ ____________________

______ ____________________

______ ____________________

20TH

JULY

#

#

#

AUGUST

#

#

#

SEPTEMBER

#

#

#

OCTOBER

#

#

#

NOVEMBER

#

#

#

DECEMBER

#

#

#

Only be careful, and watch yourselves closely so that you do not forget the things your eyes have seen or let them fade from your heart as long as you live.

Deuteronomy 4:9

21

grace glimpse

Seeing Grace

Then the Lord told him, "Make a replica of a poisonous snake and attach it to a pole. All who are bitten will live if they simply look at it!" So Moses made a snake out of bronze and attached it to a pole. Then anyone who was bitten by a snake could look at the bronze snake and be healed!

Numbers 21:8–9 NLT

First the eyes. Always first, the inner eyes.

"Looking comes first," wrote C. S. Lewis.[1]

Looking is the love. Looking is evidence of the believing.

How we behold determines if we hold joy. Behold glory and be held by God.

How we look determines how we live—*if* we live.

And I'd read what Jesus said, and kept returning to what it meant: "In the same way that Moses lifted the serpent in the desert so people could have something to see and then believe, it is necessary for the Son of Man to be lifted up—and everyone who looks up to him, trusting and expectant, will gain a real life, eternal life" (John 3:14–15 MSG).

Isn't Jesus Himself saying that people need to see and then believe—that looking and believing are the same thing? That in the right inner looking, we can gain the right outer life, the *saved full* life?

I had read it and had forgotten (always!), but I remember it now: "Faith is the gaze of a soul upon a saving God."[2]

Faith is the gaze of a soul. Faith is the seeing soul's eyes upon a saving God.

That's what makes us persevere through a life: to see Him who is invisible!

Lord, You heal every infirmity. Heal my stunted sight. Open the eyes of my heart. I long to see Your heart—even when I can't see Your hand. The remedy is in the retina.

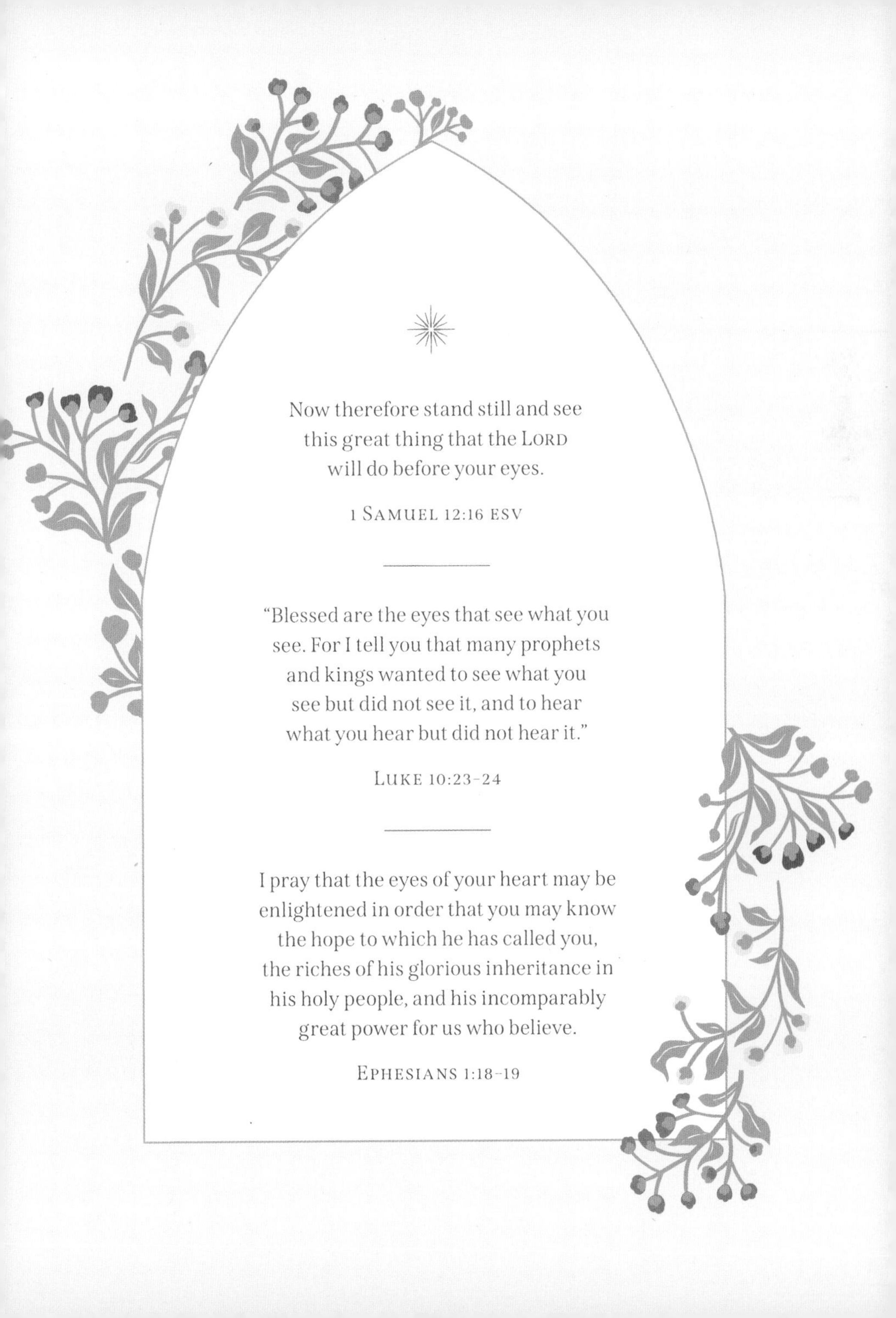

Now therefore stand still and see
this great thing that the LORD
will do before your eyes.

1 SAMUEL 12:16 ESV

"Blessed are the eyes that see what you
see. For I tell you that many prophets
and kings wanted to see what you
see but did not see it, and to hear
what you hear but did not hear it."

LUKE 10:23–24

I pray that the eyes of your heart may be
enlightened in order that you may know
the hope to which he has called you,
the riches of his glorious inheritance in
his holy people, and his incomparably
great power for us who believe.

EPHESIANS 1:18–19

Gifts & Gratitudes

JANUARY

#

#

#

FEBRUARY

#

#

#

MARCH

#

#

#

APRIL

#

#

#

MAY

#

#

#

JUNE

#

#

#

21st

JULY

#

#

#

AUGUST

#

#

#

SEPTEMBER

#

#

#

OCTOBER

#

#

#

NOVEMBER

#

#

#

DECEMBER

#

#

#

Ask and it will be given to you; seek and you will find; knock and the door will be opened to you. For everyone who asks receives; the one who seeks finds; and to the one who knocks, the door will be opened.

MATTHEW 7:7–8

22

grace glimpse

Hunting Grace

My cup overflows. Surely your goodness and love will follow me all the days of my life, and I will dwell in the house of the LORD forever.

PSALM 23:5–6

For years, when one of the kids brought in a fistful of Queen Anne's lace, summer's scattered doilies, it was then I'd slip a vase off the shelf for the gathered flowers.

Or when our boys raced in with the first profusion of wild daffodils from the ditches, or when my farmer husband would stop the tractor at the edge of the side road and fill his arms with tiger lilies growing, carrying flowers home as a surprise.

I'd only get a vase down then.

Because the way I thought was like this:

Have beauty. Now must get a vessel.

But when my farming man gave me these four old crocks, all just thrift store finds, everything shifted a bit differently. Because I made these vases furniture, vases that always remained out—permanent fixtures in a house that could be wired for glory, that could hunt for beauty to fill up with.

My thinking shifted to go like this:

Have vessel. Now must find beauty.

Empty containers can make us seekers, hunters of glory, searchers of beauty and grace and goodness. I changed my thinking: I need to find grace-beauty to fill the emptiness, not bought beauty—beauty that can only be bought with me paying attention: A wildflower from the roadside. A branch from the woods, grasses growing long in the ditches, zinnias from the garden, a happy round face from the sunflower patch.

"Can I gather the flowers this week?" one of our sons asks, one hand on the back doorknob, scissors in the other hand.

"Can I go too?" Our little girl's already a flash of blond light across the kitchen.

What if we all become a motley tribe of beauty hunters? What if today, in the midst of everything tender and complicated and painful, there was a way to slow and see that the world's beauty outweighs its burdens, its grace greater than its grime?

When gratitude journals become permanent life furniture, white spaces opened wide, empty pages like cups to heaven, waiting to be filled with the color of His graces . . . something inside shifts, and we become seekers and lookers and noticers and God-hunters.

This can be a daily ceremony, this gathering of grace, joy to fill the emptiness, the glory of the Father never fading.

Lord God, You are the Hound of heaven who hunts the lost down and captures us with grace. Today, make me the hound of now who hunts for glory and captures joy with just that one word: thanks.

For where your treasure is, there
your heart will be also.

Matthew 6:21

You, God, are my God, earnestly
I seek you; I thirst for you, my
whole being longs for you.

Psalm 63:1

Look to the Lord and his strength;
seek his face always.

1 Chronicles 16:11

Gifts & Gratitudes

JANUARY

FEBRUARY

MARCH

APRIL

MAY

JUNE

22ND

JULY

#

#

#

AUGUST

#

#

#

SEPTEMBER

#

#

#

OCTOBER

#

#

#

NOVEMBER

#

#

#

DECEMBER

#

#

#

The LORD is my light and my salvation—whom shall I fear? The LORD is the stronghold of my life—of whom shall I be afraid?

PSALM 27:1

23

grace glimpse

Bridge Grace

Give thanks to him who alone does mighty miracles. His faithful love endures forever.

PSALM 136:4 NLT

This living a lifestyle of intentional gratitude becomes an unintentional test in the trustworthiness of God.

Count blessings and discover who can be counted on.

Have I not trusted in all kinds of ways, because I haven't counted all kinds of gifts?

Driving to a meeting at the church, I glance in the rearview mirror at the concrete bridge I'd just passed over, the one I've boldly driven straight across without second thought how many times, and I see truth reflecting back at me.

Every time fear freezes and worry writhes, every time I surrender to stress, aren't I, in some small way, somehow advertising my uncertainty in the reliability of God? That I really don't believe? But if I'm grateful to the Bridge Builder for the crossing of a million strong bridges, thankful for a million faithful moments, my life speaks my beliefs, and I trust Him again.

I shake my head at the blinding wonder of it: trust is the bridge from yesterday to tomorrow, built with planks of thanks.

Gratitude lays out the planks of trust.

Gratitude builds a deeper trust in God, so that you can walk the planks—from known to unknown—and know: He holds.

Giving thanks gives you the trust to walk less afraid.

Is that why the Israelites kept recounting their past—to trust God for their future? Remembering is an act of thanksgiving. Gratitude is not only the memories of our heart; gratitude is a memory of God's heart and to thank is to remember God.

Isn't this what ultimately Jesus asks of us in the Last Supper? One of the very last directives He offered to His disciples, the one of supreme import but one I too often neglect—to remember. *Do this in remembrance of Me.* Remember and give thanks.

This is the crux of Christianity—to remember and give thanks, *eucharisteo,* for who our good God is.

Because remembering with thanks is what causes us to trust—to really believe in the Giver of Grace.

Lord God, I claim Christ as my bridge back to You and I trust the Bridge Builder to hold all the moments of my life—and me. Remind me today, Lord, to give thanks to You for always holding. I am relieved of the burdens when I've believed in the Bridge Builder.

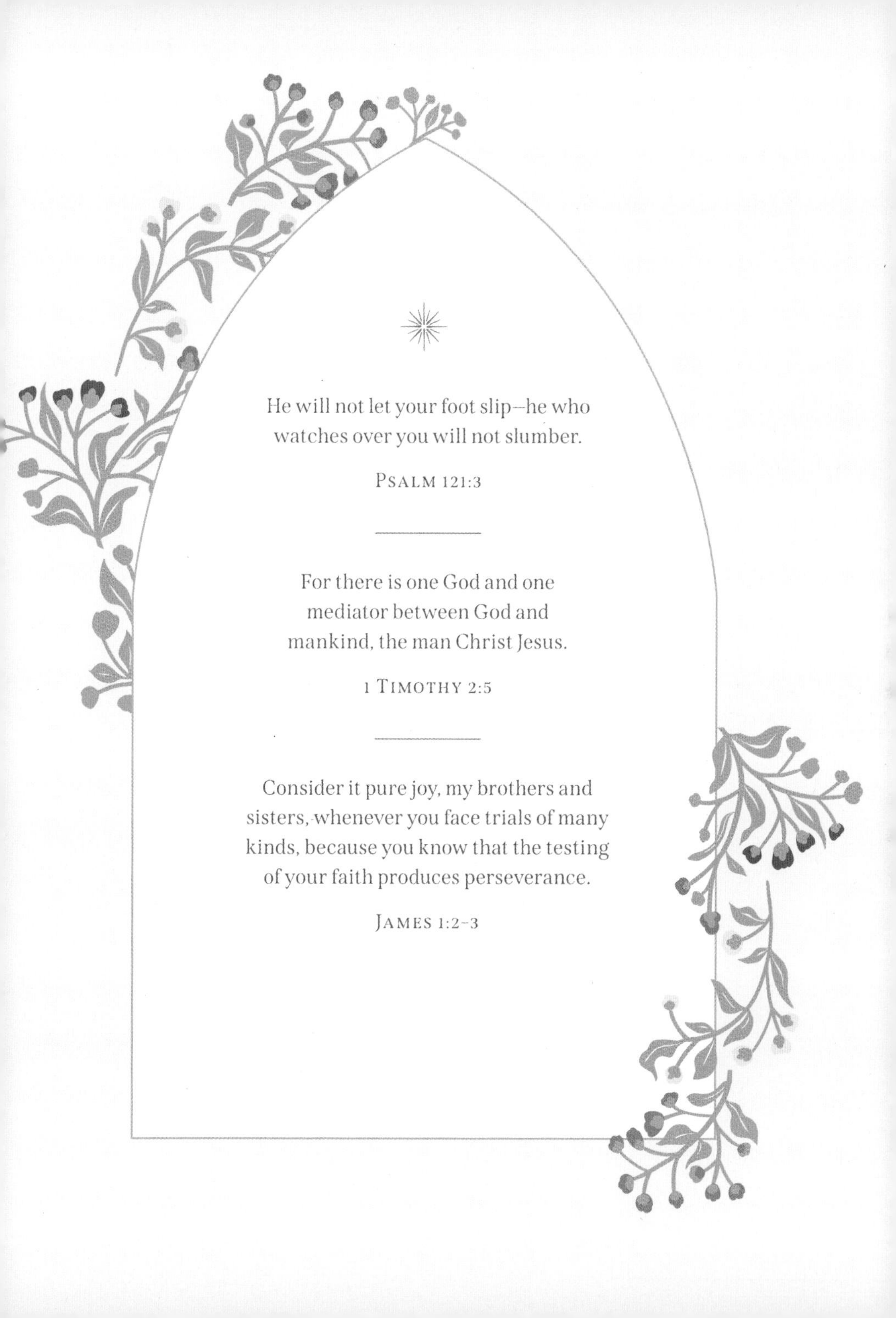

He will not let your foot slip—he who watches over you will not slumber.

PSALM 121:3

For there is one God and one mediator between God and mankind, the man Christ Jesus.

1 TIMOTHY 2:5

Consider it pure joy, my brothers and sisters, whenever you face trials of many kinds, because you know that the testing of your faith produces perseverance.

JAMES 1:2–3

Gifts & Gratitudes

JANUARY

#

#

#

FEBRUARY

#

#

#

MARCH

#

#

#

APRIL

#

#

#

MAY

#

#

#

JUNE

#

#

#

23RD

JULY

#
#
#

AUGUST

#
#
#

SEPTEMBER

#
#
#

OCTOBER

#
#
#

NOVEMBER

#
#
#

DECEMBER

#
#
#

I know what it is to be in need, and I know what it is to have plenty. I have learned the secret of being content in any and every situation, whether well fed or hungry, whether living in plenty or in want. I can do all this through him who gives me strength.

PHILIPPIANS 4:12–13

24

grace glimpse

Hard Grace

I want to know Christ—yes, to know the power of his resurrection and participation in his sufferings, becoming like him in his death.

PHILIPPIANS 3:10

There are days and seasons when I can't keep myself from saying it to God, this raw heart echo of that of Teresa of Avila: "If this is how You treat Your friends, no wonder You have so few!"[1]

Honestly? I've been David lamenting, "Why, LORD ...?" (Psalm 10:1). Why this broken world punched through with losses? "How long, LORD?" (Psalm 13:1). How long until every baby thrives and all children sleep down the hall from a mom and dad wrapped up in love, and each womb swells with vigorous life, and every single cancer clinic sits empty and we all grow old together? How long?

I know a neighboring woman folding away the clothes of her dead son, and I sit in a room full of the battered and busted and I lament: *Please.*

And He takes the empty hands and draws me close to the thrum of Love. *You may suffer loss but in Me is anything ever lost, really? Isn't everything that belongs to Christ also yours? Loved ones lost still belong to Him—then aren't they still yours? Do I not own the cattle on a thousand hills; everything? Aren't then all provisions in Christ also yours?*

If you haven't lost Christ, child, nothing is ever lost forever. Remember: "It is through many tribulations that we must enter the kingdom of God" (Acts 14:22 NASB).

Dare we trust?: the dark can give birth to life; suffering can deliver grace. Dare we believe?: *all is grace.* What if we dared to see through all the ache of this broken world to the realest reality?: *God is always good and I am always loved.*

Everything is eucharisteo. Because giving thanks, *eucharisteo,* is how Jesus, at the Last Supper, showed us how to transfigure all things—take the pain that is given, give thanks in it, and let God transform even this into a tender joy of God Himself fulfilling all emptiness with more of Himself.

This is the hard eucharisteo. This is the *hard* discipline of leaning into the ugly and painful and finding something to whisper thanks for, to transfigure even this into a redemptive beauty. This is the *hard* discipline to give thanks in all things at all times because He is all good. This is the *hard* discipline to number the griefs as grace, because as the surgeon cuts open to heal, so God chooses to cut into my ungrateful heart to make me whole.

In Christ, all is grace, only *because in Christ, all can transfigure.*

Lord, You make all grace because You transfigure all. Cause me to believe, right in the midst of hard things, that You are patiently transfiguring all the notes of my life. Let me live the hard discipline to give thanks in hard things. I lean hard on You—who softens my heart.

Come to me, all you who are weary and burdened, and I will give you rest.

MATTHEW 11:28

Now is your time of grief, but I will see you again and you will rejoice, and no one will take away your joy.

JOHN 16:22

He who did not spare his own Son, but gave him up for us all—how will he not also, along with him, graciously give us all things?

ROMANS 8:32

Gifts & Gratitudes

JANUARY

#

#

#

FEBRUARY

#

#

#

MARCH

#

#

#

APRIL

#

#

#

MAY

#

#

#

JUNE

#

#

#

24TH

JULY

#

#

#

AUGUST

#

#

#

SEPTEMBER

#

#

#

OCTOBER

#

#

#

NOVEMBER

#

#

#

DECEMBER

#

#

#

As the rain and the snow come down from heaven, and do not return to it without watering the earth and making it bud and flourish, so that it yields seed for the sower and bread for the eater, so is my word that goes out from my mouth: It will not return to me empty, but will accomplish what I desire and achieve the purpose for which I sent it. You will go out in joy and be led forth in peace; the mountains and hills will burst into song before you, and all the trees of the field will clap their hands.

ISAIAH 55:10–12

This-Moment Grace

The life of mortals is like grass, they flourish like a flower of the field. . . . But from everlasting to everlasting the LORD*'s love is with those who fear him, and his righteousness with their children's children.*

PSALM 103:15, 17

It falls unexpected on a day in late fall.

A snow-white whisper hushing the trees burnt all red.

A lone woman stands at a window and I watch the snow fall behind her, her at the glass, and the flakes so soundless, heaven on white wing.

And I don't expect it, in a room full of women and flashing laughter, the way she turns and says it quiet to me—"My daughter is dying."

Is there really anything to murmur except to just come close and stand with someone?

She says it straight out and clear. "But there have been gifts."

That when the diagnosis came, the doctor said terminal and only a year more, at the most five—but then the unexpected, this wild grace of ten whole years.

How she once sang like a bird, twirled in her four-year-old spin, and then the years of slow regression, the walking giving way to the wheelchair, the songs giving way to loss of words, and now, giving way to infant beginnings.

"It's all kept us always living just in this moment—because we know today is the last like this." Sometimes you know you will never forget the way the light burns in someone's eyes.

She's a flame in snow.

"Just always so grateful for every moment we've been given." The snow's now falling straight down behind her.

Each day is a gift that might not have been. Each day is a gift that doesn't assume there will be the gift of another.

I reach out, just to tenderly touch her shoulder, and she's radiant and the truth lands here in the open hands: giving thanks to God for what is, is what ushers one into the very presence of God, who is right here.

And this is why He asks us to always give thanks.

He comes to be with those with the open, grateful hands for all the miracles of grace that might never have been.

In the morning the white-laced water begins its melt, these days all vapor.

Her testament, it remains, and I remember the way she flashed grace in snow, one fading moment after another, and I want to ignite with gratitude all these gifts that might never have been.

God, today is the last like this. This place, these people, this moment—it will never again be just like this. Cause my eyes to see everything in my life afresh. I may not pass by here again. Now is not a forever grace, but amazing grace.

Why, you do not even know what will happen tomorrow. What is your life? You are a mist that appears for a little while and then vanishes.

JAMES 4:14

He will wipe away every tear from their eyes, and death shall be no more, neither shall there be mourning, nor crying, nor pain anymore, for the former things have passed away.

REVELATION 21:4 ESV

Gifts & Gratitudes

JANUARY

______ ____________________

______ ____________________

______ ____________________

FEBRUARY

______ ____________________

______ ____________________

______ ____________________

MARCH

______ ____________________

______ ____________________

______ ____________________

APRIL

______ ____________________

______ ____________________

______ ____________________

MAY

______ ____________________

______ ____________________

______ ____________________

JUNE

______ ____________________

______ ____________________

______ ____________________

25TH

JULY

#

#

#

AUGUST

#

#

#

SEPTEMBER

#

#

#

OCTOBER

#

#

#

NOVEMBER

#

#

#

DECEMBER

#

#

#

"Are not two sparrows sold for a penny? Yet not one of them will fall to the ground outside your Father's care."

MATTHEW 10:29

26

grace glimpse

Small Grace

"Truly I tell you, unless you change and become like little children, you will never enter the kingdom of heaven. Therefore, whoever takes the lowly position of this child is the greatest in the kingdom of heaven."

MATTHEW 18:3–4

Our little girl's laughter makes me laugh too, and I can hear her going through the house, gleefully recording all time and space with an old point-and-shoot camera. Child and mother, we've exchanged places.

Eventually, she comes looking for me, her face filled with lens, her every step activating another click. I'm separating whites from darks in the laundry room.

"Can you show all the pictures back to me now?" She holds the camera out to me, as long as the neck strap will allow. Nothing can restrain her giddiness.

Settling into a pile of laundry, our heads lean toward each other and touch. Her arm around my neck, we scroll through her photos on the glowing screen. A picture of me bent over her, showing her which button to press. I'm a mountain over her lens. I can feel the laughter rising up in her, and she cups her hand over her mouth to catch the bubbling pleasure. She's enchanted by her photos. I grin.

Frame of a table. A doorknob. A bookshelf skewed on a tilt.

Yet her photos surprise, every single one. Why? It takes me a moment to make sense of it—it's the vantage point. At thirty-six inches, her height presents an angle that is unfamiliar to me and utterly captivating: The study ceiling arches like a dome, her bed a floating barge. The stairs plunge like a gorge. She's Alice in Wonderland, all the world grown Everest-like around and above her.

"Do you like them, Mama?" She pats my cheek with her laughter-drenched hand.

I can only murmur, flicking through her gallery. "Marvelous . . . just marvelous."

She giggles, and I lay the camera aside and tickle her soft belly and she throws her head back, bliss, and I kiss our sweet little girl, and she laughs, breathless.

I want this kind of crazy, happy joy, God. How to see the world again through eyes like hers? To live in the wide-eyed wonder of a world where you are small and the world around you is larger than life, so otherworldly?

As G. K. Chesterton wrote, "How much larger your life would be if your self could become smaller in it."[1]

When you live small and in awe, you experience this great joy in God.

Dear Lord, make me decrease that You may increase and keep me small and humble. Cause me to embrace that simplest of truths—that all wonder and worship can only grow out of smallness.

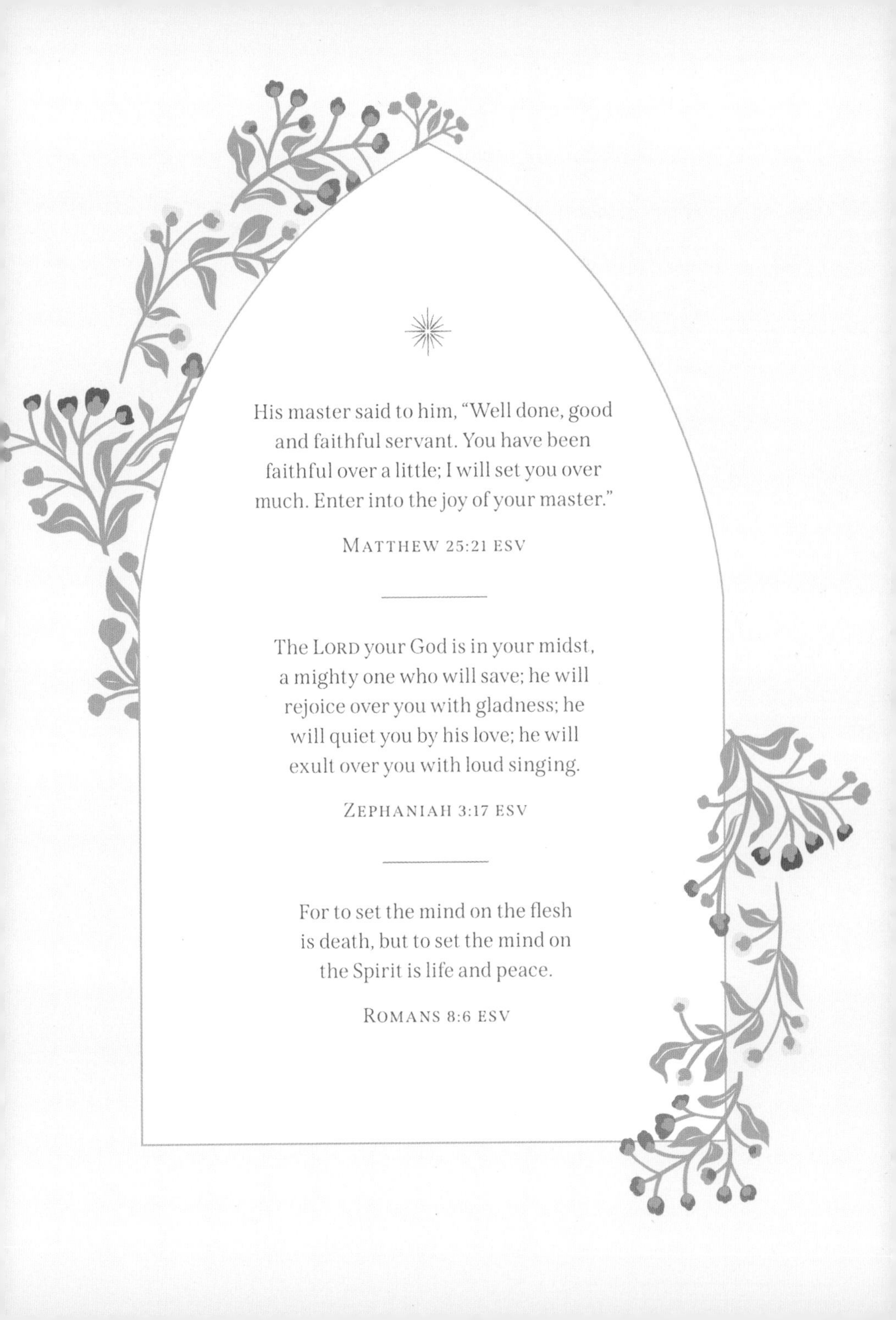

His master said to him, "Well done, good and faithful servant. You have been faithful over a little; I will set you over much. Enter into the joy of your master."

MATTHEW 25:21 ESV

The LORD your God is in your midst, a mighty one who will save; he will rejoice over you with gladness; he will quiet you by his love; he will exult over you with loud singing.

ZEPHANIAH 3:17 ESV

For to set the mind on the flesh is death, but to set the mind on the Spirit is life and peace.

ROMANS 8:6 ESV

Gifts & Gratitudes

JANUARY

\# ________ ________________________________

\# ________ ________________________________

\# ________ ________________________________

FEBRUARY

\# ________ ________________________________

\# ________ ________________________________

\# ________ ________________________________

MARCH

\# ________ ________________________________

\# ________ ________________________________

\# ________ ________________________________

APRIL

\# ________ ________________________________

\# ________ ________________________________

\# ________ ________________________________

MAY

\# ________ ________________________________

\# ________ ________________________________

\# ________ ________________________________

JUNE

\# ________ ________________________________

\# ________ ________________________________

\# ________ ________________________________

26TH

JULY

#
#
#

AUGUST

#
#
#

SEPTEMBER

#
#
#

OCTOBER

#
#
#

NOVEMBER

#
#
#

DECEMBER

#
#
#

Humility is the fear of the LORD; its wages
are riches and honor and life.
PROVERBS 22:4

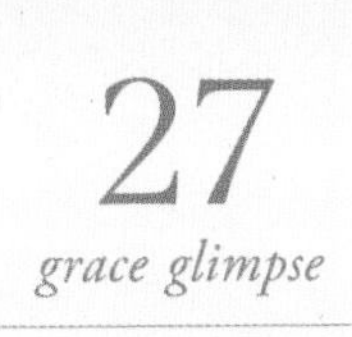

27

grace glimpse

Humble Grace

"God blesses those who are humble, for they will inherit the whole earth."

MATTHEW 5:5 NLT

I think of it only countless times a year, that single wide-eyed night by the bed of one of our sons in the pediatric wing of a city hospital. The moaning of babes, the crying of sick children, the murmur of nurses with grim prognoses on lips. I did not sleep that night, the pain of that place begging me to pray and keep praying.

After our son was given the thumbs-up following his surgery and his doctor's signature to be released, I came home to bedrooms and bathrooms and kitchen and fridge and windows and unmerited health and I threw up my arms in relieved gratitude.

Here? This place? All a gift! All an unmerited gift!

All things but forty-eight hours earlier I entirely took for granted—that

I even rather half resented as flawed and less than—I spun around: *All flattening grace!* And there has not been a single night in the years since, that I haven't whispered in bedside prayers for those who cry out in the dark, for we witnessed and we remember and we will always carry. . . .

Is it only when our lives are emptied that we're flattened with gratitude by how truly full our lives were?

Instead of filling with expectations, the joy-filled expect nothing—and are filled.

This breath! This oak tree! This daisy! This work! This sky! These people! This place! *This day! Unmerited grace! Surprising grace!*

C. S. Lewis said he was "surprised by joy." Perhaps there is no way to discover joy but as surprise, as unexpected amazing grace? This, the way the small live. Every day.

Yes, the small even have a biblical nomenclature. Doesn't God call them the *humble*?

The *humble* live surprised by unmerited grace.

The *humble* live by grateful joy.

Lord, I repent of it all: The expectations that kill relationships and the entitlement that steals all joy. Please, Lord, today, make me small and surprised by staggering grace! Make me remember that humility comes before happiness.

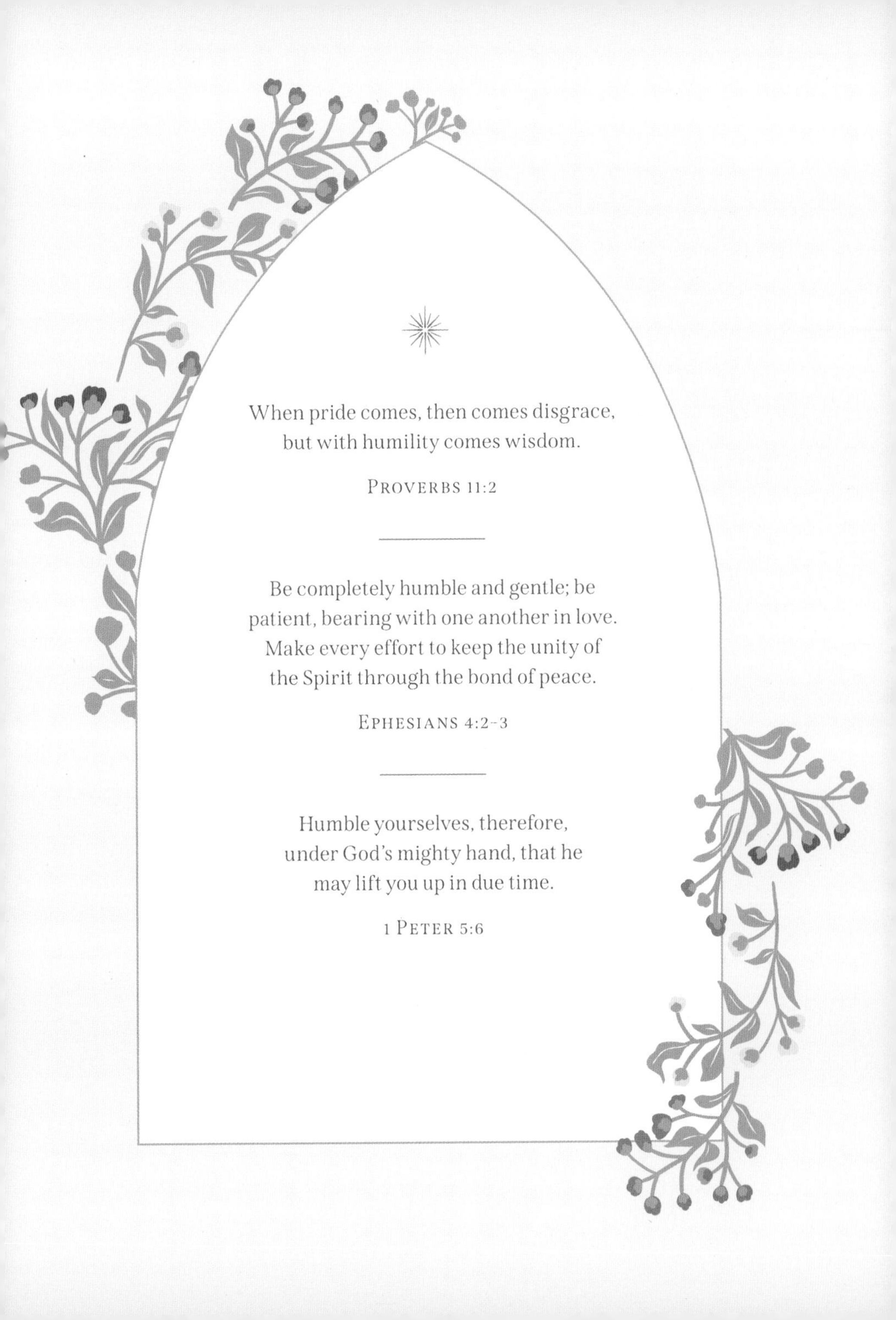

When pride comes, then comes disgrace,
but with humility comes wisdom.

PROVERBS 11:2

Be completely humble and gentle; be
patient, bearing with one another in love.
Make every effort to keep the unity of
the Spirit through the bond of peace.

EPHESIANS 4:2–3

Humble yourselves, therefore,
under God's mighty hand, that he
may lift you up in due time.

1 PETER 5:6

Gifts & Gratitudes

JANUARY

______ ______________________________

______ ______________________________

______ ______________________________

FEBRUARY

______ ______________________________

______ ______________________________

______ ______________________________

MARCH

______ ______________________________

______ ______________________________

______ ______________________________

APRIL

______ ______________________________

______ ______________________________

______ ______________________________

MAY

______ ______________________________

______ ______________________________

______ ______________________________

JUNE

______ ______________________________

______ ______________________________

______ ______________________________

27TH

JULY

#

#

#

AUGUST

#

#

#

SEPTEMBER

#

#

#

OCTOBER

#

#

#

NOVEMBER

#

#

#

DECEMBER

#

#

#

Whoever sows to please their flesh, from the flesh will reap destruction; whoever sows to please the Spirit, from the Spirit will reap eternal life. Let us not become weary in doing good, for at the proper time we will reap a harvest if we do not give up.

GALATIANS 6:8–9

28

grace glimpse

Seed Grace

"Behold, I have given you every plant yielding seed that is on the face of all the earth, and every tree with seed in its fruit. You shall have them for food."

GENESIS 1:29 ESV

Don't drop any of the seeds." Our son Levi leans over his older brother Caleb's shoulder.

"Joshua, can you bring another spade?" I call to our second son across the lane. We're breaking the earth open, making a garden in front of the barn, and it's making something in me heal.

I tear open the seed packets of zucchini, and is it this, too, witnessing how God gives impossible gifts and asks for wild faith? The seeds, they fall into my hand, small jewels. I am holding seeds, like the first gift God ever bestowed upon His people, back in the Garden of Eden.

But how do you look at seeds and believe He will feed us, when what He gives doesn't look like near enough? When it looks like less than a handful instead of a plateful, or a year full, or a life full? When it looks inedible?

These seeds—how in the world do they become food? Small seeds can look like a bit of a joke. To hand someone seeds for pangs of starvation, and ask one to believe in a coming feast—is this what everyday faith is?

Behold! For those who have learned to see—He gives, He gifts, He gives good gifts. He gifts with seeds as small as moments, grace upon grace, and the unlikely here and now, it shall sustain you, feed you.

Do not disdain the small. Gratitude for the seemingly insignificant—a seed—plants the giant miracle. The whole of life—even the hard—is made up of the minute parts, and if we miss the infinitesimals, we miss the whole.

There is a way to live the big of giving thanks in all things and it is this: To give thanks in this one small thing. The moments will add up.

Our son Joshua, he brings me a spade. He begins on one long row of lettuce. I plant gladioli bulbs. Levi scratches out his lines of sweet corn. Shalom pours her watering can careful over tomatoes that Hope's tucking into earth. Caleb hills up for pumpkins. We're all just ragamuffins out here, hunched over our wild song of faith: *Holy, Holy, Holy . . .*

We can pray bent not only in sanctuary, but over soil, and we can bow over seed rows, not only in pews.

And if prayers are what we seed and cross-love is what we knead, what we reap and what we eat is the harvest of God. He is enough, with all these small moments of grace.

Lord, what would happen today if I saw all the not-enough, too-little in my life to be but a seed? All the hardly-things could be holy-things—small somethings You are growing into more glory for You. Cause me to believe again: all feasts began as seeds.

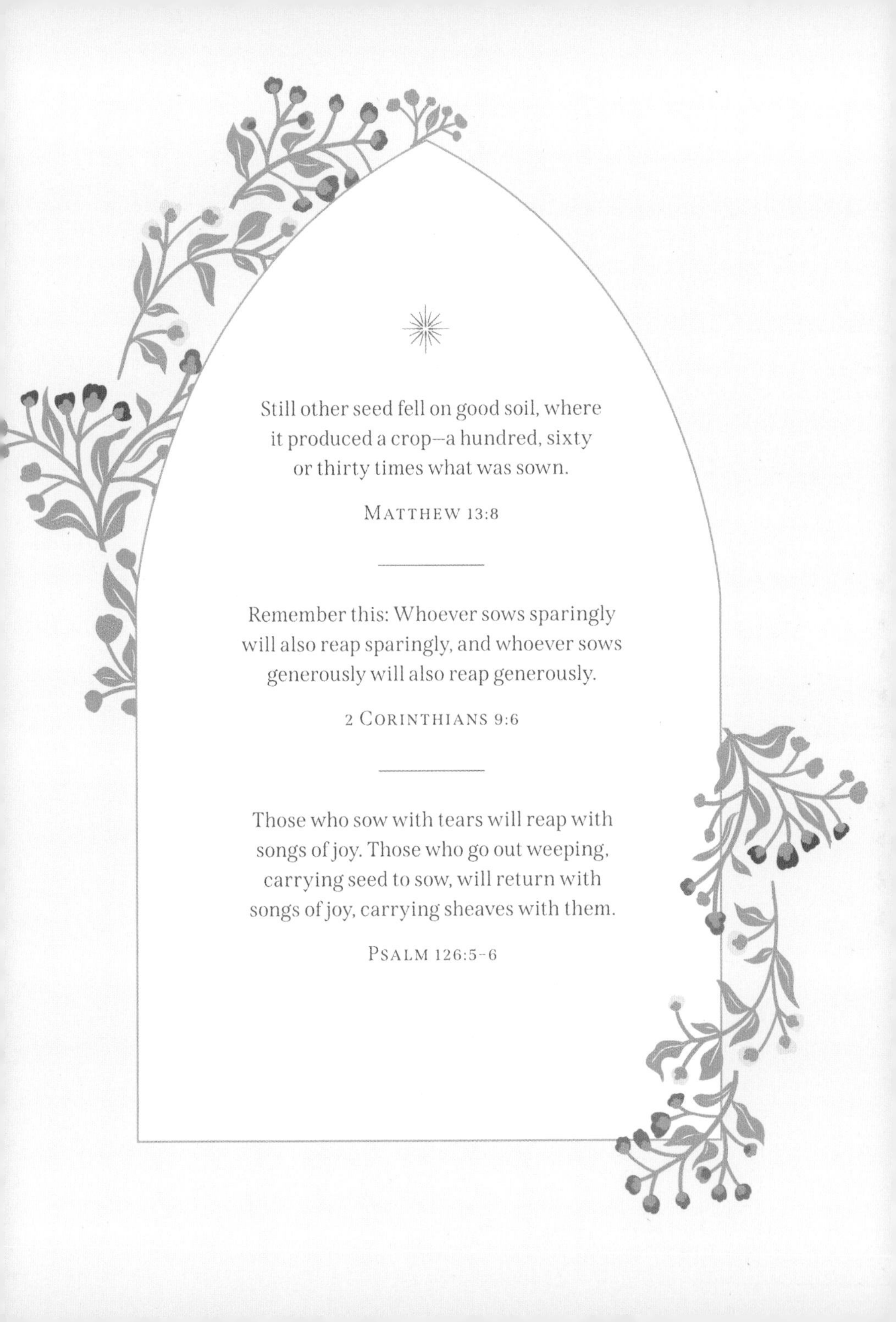

Still other seed fell on good soil, where
it produced a crop—a hundred, sixty
or thirty times what was sown.

MATTHEW 13:8

Remember this: Whoever sows sparingly
will also reap sparingly, and whoever sows
generously will also reap generously.

2 CORINTHIANS 9:6

Those who sow with tears will reap with
songs of joy. Those who go out weeping,
carrying seed to sow, will return with
songs of joy, carrying sheaves with them.

PSALM 126:5–6

Gifts & Gratitudes

JANUARY

#

#

#

FEBRUARY

#

#

#

MARCH

#

#

#

APRIL

#

#

#

MAY

#

#

#

JUNE

#

#

#

28TH

JULY

#

#

#

AUGUST

#

#

#

SEPTEMBER

#

#

#

OCTOBER

#

#

#

NOVEMBER

#

#

#

DECEMBER

#

#

#

May your unfailing love come to me, Lord,
your salvation, according to your promise.

Psalm 119:41

29

grace glimpse

Wedded Grace

"A man leaves his father and mother and is joined to his wife, and the two are united into one." This is a great mystery, but it is an illustration of the way Christ and the church are one.

EPHESIANS 5:31–32 NLT

When the back door of the sanctuary opens and the bride floats down the aisle under that veil of white, the groom grins giddy.

A son leans down the pew and whispers it too loud to me: "The guy looks like he's going to split, he's so happy."

My farmer husband squeezes my hand, and murmurs in my ear. "We should go home and recite our vows again too."

The next Sunday morning, we sit in the pews of our chapel, and the preacher's preaching who we are in Christ.

"In Christ, you have immediate access to God and all of this is yours—joy, acceptance, completeness, rest, righteousness, access to the throne of God. You are sealed and He has pledged Himself to His people, and you are His."

And I look around and it strikes me—why aren't we all grinning giddy? Why aren't we, like that groom, all smiling like we just might split?

I keep reading the vows the preacher has on the screen, slow and captivated. God's given all these gifts to all His children, no matter where we are—why not revel in this, because what love is greater than this?

- *Joy is yours.* "Though you have not seen Him, you love Him, and though you do not see Him now, but believe in Him, you greatly rejoice with joy inexpressible and full of glory" (1 Peter 1:8 *NASB*).
- *Acceptance is yours.* "To the praise of the glory of his grace, wherein he hath made us accepted in the beloved" (Ephesians 1:6 *KJV*).
- *Completeness is yours.* "And in Him you have been made complete" (Colossians 2:10 *NASB*).

Why don't our cheeks hurt with the happiness of it all?

The vows of the Christ, they are covenant, and He lasts when we lose everything else, and *all* the gifts are *in Christ alone.*

When the Farmer asks me on the way home why I'm smiling, I squeeze his hand, murmur something about how I just can't stop, the promise of all these gifts in Christ moving me into a deeper sense of joy.

Lord God, today, make me giddy with gratitude for Your covenanted gifts—all joy, all acceptance, all completeness, all in Christ.

And I saw the holy city, new Jerusalem, coming down out of heaven from God, prepared as a bride adorned for her husband.

REVELATION 21:2 ESV

Now you are the body of Christ, and each one of you is a part of it.

1 CORINTHIANS 12:27

Once you were not a people; but now you are the people of God.

1 PETER 2:10

Gifts & Gratitudes

JANUARY

#

#

#

FEBRUARY

#

#

#

MARCH

#

#

#

APRIL

#

#

#

MAY

#

#

#

JUNE

#

#

#

29TH

JULY

#

#

#

AUGUST

#

#

#

SEPTEMBER

#

#

#

OCTOBER

#

#

#

NOVEMBER

#

#

#

DECEMBER

#

#

#

"Therefore everyone who hears these words of mine and puts them into practice is like a wise man who built his house on the rock."
MATTHEW 7:24

Standing Grace

No longer will violence be heard in your land, nor ruin or destruction within your borders, but you will call your walls Salvation and your gates Praise.

ISAIAH 60:18

Down by the water's edge our boys build a sandcastle. Caleb wields his shovel like a man with a back built for trenches. Levi hauls up pails of water from the shore and he pours.

Kai and Joshua dribble the sand straight from their fingers, sculpting. The walls grow higher. They keep at it, building and forming. Or this happens—the sand settles, sinks. Crumbles. It's always happening like that on the beach—nothing stands still, the moments always moving in a direction.

And it is like that with our words. The way sand moves, our every word's moving either one way or the other—words either raising Christ or building self higher.

Words praising Him . . . or wrangling to be praised ourselves.

There's always either this seeping of bitterness or our lives being straight spires of gratitude for blessings.

"I need more water, Levi—or it's going to fall." Joshua curves over his section of sand wall like a prayer.

How can our life stand, our homes stand, how can our inner and outer walls stand? Unless we make it a habit to give thanks, is it possible that we habitually give our people grief? Unless we consistently speak praise, is it possible that we consistently speak a kind of poison to our people? Unless we are intentional about giving God glory throughout the day, is it possible that our days unintentionally give way to grumbling?

"Levi—it's crumbling over here!" Kai turns quick. He's looking beyond himself, looking for help. It's only when we focus on the Christic-center of everything that everything finds its center and walls stand.

It's in praising our Savior in all things that we are saved from discouragement in all things.

"Thanks, Levi, thanks." Kai pats more sand in cracks and Levi tilts the pail, and kneeling together, they bridge the gap.

"Oh yeah, Levi, yeah—*thank you.*"

Does it always come down to just two ways to do life? Do doxology—or do destruction? From here, where I'm trying to build a life, I watch how they build their house, one thanks at a time.

Father God, make me speak praise today, not poison; make me intentionally give You glory throughout the day, that my day doesn't unintentionally crumble in grumbling. In thanking You in all things, I am saved from discouragement in all things, and this today is my earnest prayer: make me do doxology, not destruction.

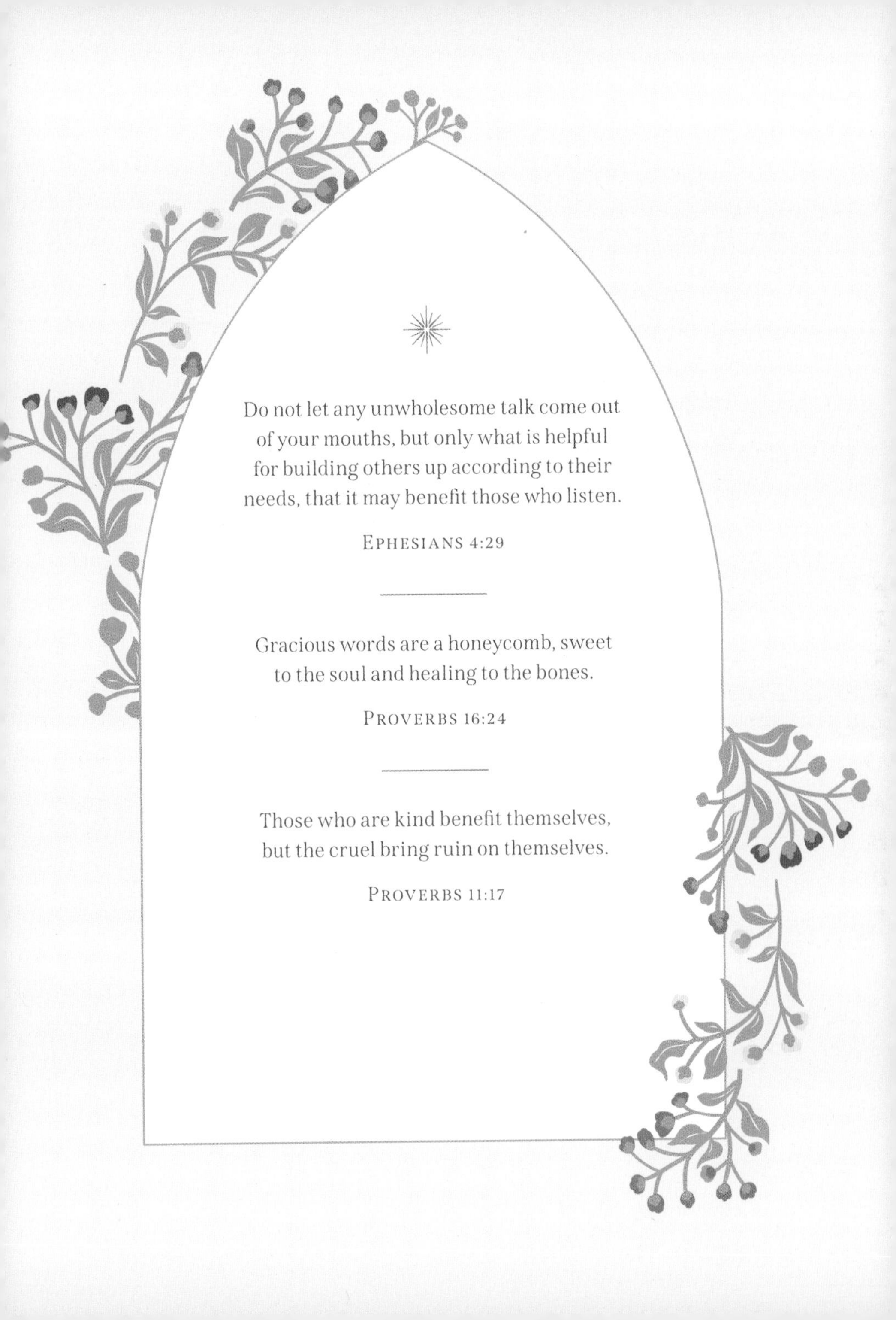

Do not let any unwholesome talk come out of your mouths, but only what is helpful for building others up according to their needs, that it may benefit those who listen.

EPHESIANS 4:29

Gracious words are a honeycomb, sweet to the soul and healing to the bones.

PROVERBS 16:24

Those who are kind benefit themselves, but the cruel bring ruin on themselves.

PROVERBS 11:17

Gifts & Gratitudes

JANUARY

#

#

#

FEBRUARY

#

#

#

MARCH

#

#

#

APRIL

#

#

#

MAY

#

#

#

JUNE

#

#

#

30TH

JULY

#

#

#

AUGUST

#

#

#

SEPTEMBER

#

#

#

OCTOBER

#

#

#

NOVEMBER

#

#

#

DECEMBER

#

#

#

Oh, taste and see that the Lord is good!
Blessed is the man who takes refuge in him!

Psalm 34:8 ESV

Happiest Grace

For the sin of this one man, Adam, brought death to many. But even greater is God's wonderful grace and his gift of forgiveness to many through this other man, Jesus Christ.

ROMANS 5:15 NLT

During the hour drive it takes to get to the lake on a drowsy Sunday afternoon, I think of the sermon we'd heard that morning. The preacher preaching pure gospel and how to be born again.

Twenty-five years he's been preaching it in our little country chapel, to the hog farmers, the corn croppers, the mothers with babies in arms. How you can't work for God's love, angle for it, or jockey for it–you can't earn God's love. *You can only turn toward God's love.*

When we all unpile up at the lake, and the kids run toward the water, my mama and I, we stand there, toes in sand and the wind hair.

Our faces turned right toward the sun.

It's a gift, the preacher said. Salvation *is* the gift, the one wrapped in God taking on skin, laying His bare love out for the world, arms spreading to the very ends of the limbs of the tree of life.

There is all the kids' laughter. There is their running. There is my radiant mama smiling. There is this singular seagull writing across the sky. These are gifts, all *gifts.*

Holy joy lies in the habit of murmuring thanks to God for the smallest of graces. I often falter, but this is the habit to wear for a lifetime.

And really? Christ is the offering and salvation is the gift and repentance is what makes us recipients of grace. *Christ* is the gift. *Christ* is the bridge home. *Christ* is our joy. There is only one gift—the one ocean of Christ that falls as rain over us in a thousand ways. How can I forget this, ever stop giving thanks for Him alone?

Happiness is not getting something but being given to Someone.

It is the sacrifice of Christ that returns us to God and communion with Him is possible anywhere and bless the Lord, oh, my soul, bless the very Maker of my soul.

Water keeps washing up over my toes.

All the waves keep rushing up to meet the feet turned.

And as the sun sets, I watch a father catching his laughing girl . . . and I feel it all, all this happiness . . . just in Him, right until the very last light.

Oh God, my God, holy joy lies in the habit of murmuring thanks to You for the smallest of graces. Forgive my faltering and make this thanksgiving to You the habit I'll wear all my life. Because You, my Lord and Savior, You are the one Gift, the one Bridge—the one Ocean that falls as rain over me in a thousand ways. Kindle my heart again, to know that happiness is not getting something but being given to Someone.

Out of his fullness we have all received grace in place of grace already given.

John 1:16

See what great love the Father has lavished on us, that we should be called children of God!

1 John 3:1

Happy *are* the people who are in such a state; Happy *are* the people whose God *is* the Lord!

Psalm 144:15 NKJV

Gifts & Gratitudes

JANUARY

______ ______________________________

______ ______________________________

______ ______________________________

FEBRUARY

______ ______________________________

______ ______________________________

______ ______________________________

MARCH

______ ______________________________

______ ______________________________

______ ______________________________

APRIL

______ ______________________________

______ ______________________________

______ ______________________________

MAY

______ ______________________________

______ ______________________________

______ ______________________________

JUNE

______ ______________________________

______ ______________________________

______ ______________________________

31ST

JULY

#

#

#

AUGUST

#

#

#

SEPTEMBER

#

#

#

OCTOBER

#

#

#

NOVEMBER

#

#

#

DECEMBER

#

#

#

Notes

GRACE GLIMPSE 3: FIRST GRACE

1. Mark Buchanan, *The Holy Wild* (Colorado Springs: Multnomah, 2005), 105.

GRACE GLIMPSE 4: THINKING GRACE

1. Gilbert Keith Chesterton, *A Short History of England* (Teddington, Middlesex, UK: Echo Library, 2008), 30.

GRACE GLIMPSE 6: ANTI-ANXIETY GRACE

1. Belden Lane, *Ravished by Beauty: The Surprising Legacy of Reformed Spirituality* (New York: Oxford University Press, 2011), 65.
2. Ibid., 66.
3. Ibid.

GRACE GLIMPSE 8: SLOWING GRACE

1. Mark Buchanan, *The Rest of God: Restoring Your Soul by Restoring Your Sabbath* (Nashville: Nelson, 2007), 45, emphasis added.

GRACE GLIMPSE 15: NAMING GRACE

1. John Piper, *When I Don't Desire God: How to Fight for Joy* (Wheaton, IL: Crossway, 2004), 124.

GRACE GLIMPSE 18: HAMMERING GRACE

1. Desiderius Erasmus, *"Diluculum,* or The Early Rising," in *The Colloquies of Erasmus* (London: Reeves and Turner, 1878), 2:212.

GRACE GLIMPSE 19: AWAKENING GRACE

1. "New Letters of R. L. Stevenson," in *Harper's Monthly Magazine,* vol. 104, eds. Henry Mills Alden, Thomas Bucklin Wells, and Lee Foster Hartman (New York: Harper, 1902), 126.

GRACE GLIMPSE 21: SEEING GRACE

1. C. S. Lewis, *The Great Divorce* (New York: Macmillan, 1946), 77.
2. A. W. Tozer, *The Pursuit of God* (Camp Hill, Pa.: Christian Publications, 1982), 73.

GRACE GLIMPSE 24: HARD GRACE

1. Teresa of Avila, quoted in Amy Welborn, *The Loyola Kids Book of Saints* (Chicago: Loyola, 2001), 87.

GRACE GLIMPSE 26: SMALL GRACE

1. G. K. Chesterton, *Orthodoxy* (Rockville, MD: Serenity, 2009), 19.

About the Author

Ann Voskamp is the wife of a farmer, mama to seven, and the author of the *New York Times* bestsellers *The Broken Way*, *The Greatest Gift*, *Unwrapping the Greatest Gift*, and the sixty-week *New York Times* bestseller *One Thousand Gifts: A Dare to Live Fully Right Where You Are*, which has sold more than 1.5 million copies and has been translated into more than twenty languages.

Named by *Christianity Today* as one of fifty women most shaping culture and the church today, Ann knows unspoken broken, big country skies, and an intimacy with God that touches tender places. Cofounder of ShowUpNow.com, Ann is a passionate advocate for the marginalized and oppressed around the globe, partnering with Mercy House Global, Compassion International, and artisans around the world through her fair trade community, Grace Case. She and her husband took a leap of faith to restore a 125-year-old stone church into The Village Table—a place where everyone has a seat and knows they belong. Join the journey at www.annvoskamp.com or instagram/annvoskamp.

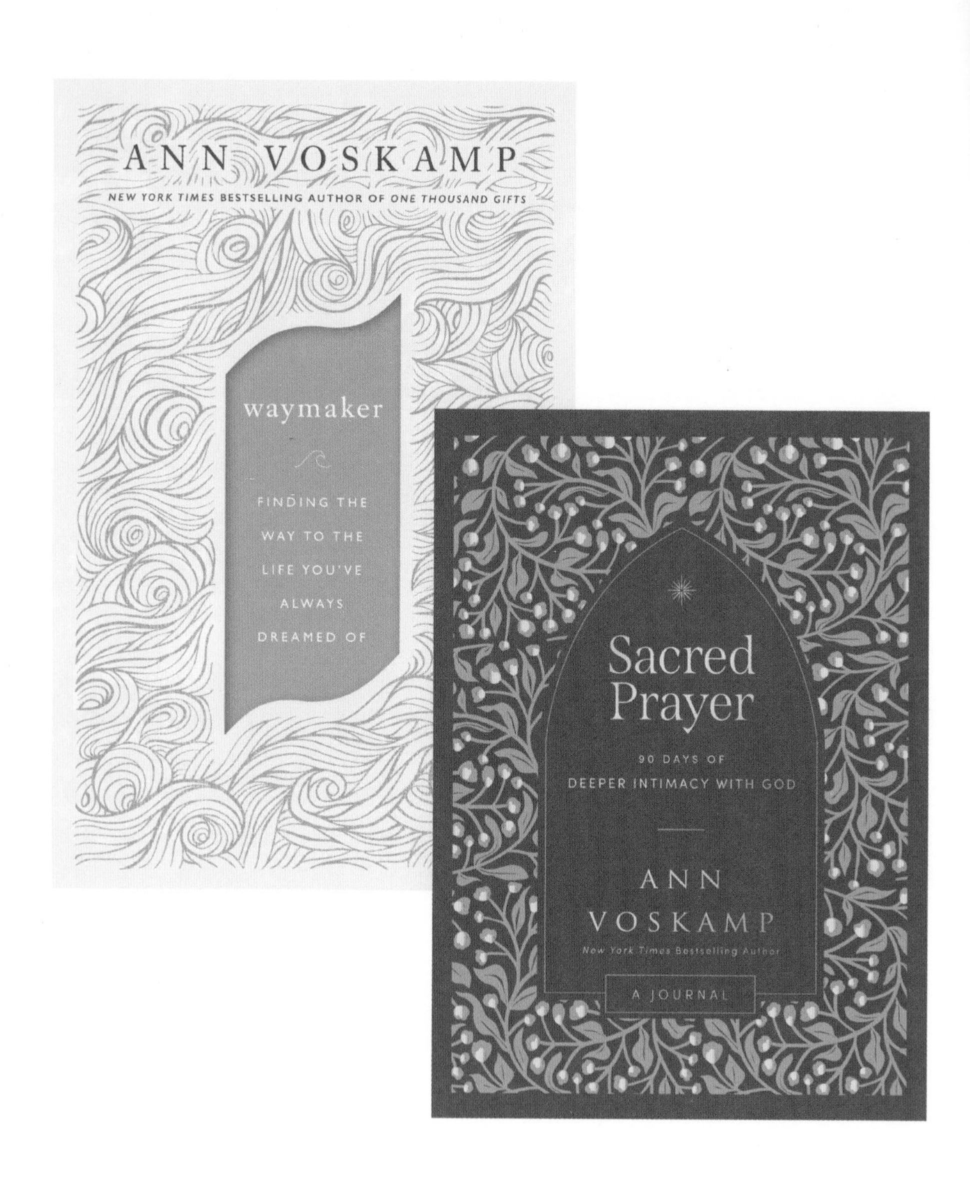
ANN VOSKAMP
NEW YORK TIMES BESTSELLING AUTHOR OF ONE THOUSAND GIFTS
waymaker
FINDING THE WAY TO THE LIFE YOU'VE ALWAYS DREAMED OF
Sacred Prayer
90 DAYS OF DEEPER INTIMACY WITH GOD
ANN VOSKAMP
New York Times Bestselling Author
A JOURNAL

VIDEO STUDY FOR YOUR CHURCH OR SMALL GROUP

If you've enjoyed the book, now you can go deeper with the *WayMaker* Bible study.

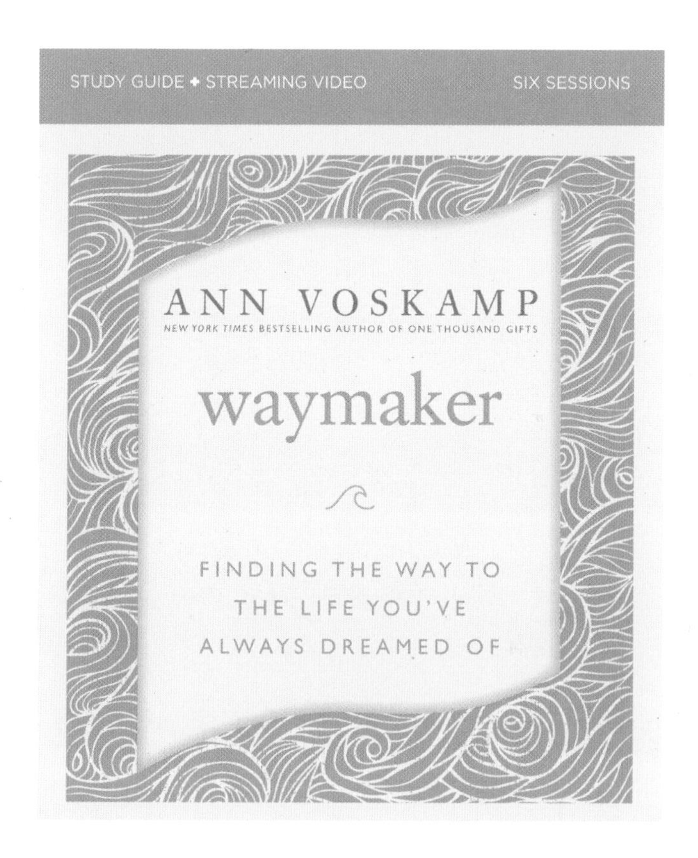

How do you navigate through the pounding storms of life with an internal calm and peace that is anchored and unwavering? Join Ann Voskamp as she teaches you the acronym SACRED as a daily habit, a compass that reorients you in relation to God.